The Complete Book of

Alternate Tunings

By Mark Hanson

Published by:

ACCENT ON MUSIC
19363 Willamette Dr. #252
West Linn, OR 97068 USA

First Printing 1995 10 9 8 7 6 5 4 3 2 1
Printed in the United States of America.

Library of Congress Catalogue in Publication Data
Hanson, Mark D. 1951-
The Complete Book of Alternate Tunings
1. Guitar—Methods—Self-Instruction. I. Title.

ISBN 0-936799-13-7 Paperback

Table of Contents

Introduction

Welcome to *The Complete Book of Alternate Tunings*. The world of alternate tunings is an exciting one. Retuning the strings on your guitar can provide beautiful sonorities that you may never have known existed. Alternate tunings also can provide a playability that is difficult to match in standard tuning. Some of the world's greatest guitarists retune their strings regularly.

This *is* an exciting world for guitarists, but one that requires some thought before entering it. Let me take a moment to explain a few things that will make it easier for you to digest this information.

What Is An "Alternate Tuning"?

For the purposes of this book, an alternate tuning is any guitar tuning other than standard. Some folks differentiate between "alternate" tunings and "open" tunings." Let me explain using a little history.

By the 1800s, "standard" tuning for the six-string guitar was E A d g b e´, lowest pitch to highest. This differed from "lute" tuning of earlier centuries, which had a lowered third string, making the modern-day equivalent E A d f# b e´. Even though E A d g b e´ was considered standard, there are published pieces from the 19th century using open-chord tunings as well. The Open D (D A d f# a d´; often referred to as "Vestapol") and Open G (D G d g b d´; often referred to as "Spanish") tunings are well documented in the 1800s.

These open-chord tunings allowed guitarists to play the instrument with a minimum of effort; indeed, no effort at all was required on the part of the fretting hand to play a basic, nice sounding chord. Other chords could be played with the use of one finger of the fretting hand, or, in the case of blues players, with the use of a slide. On an elementary level, these tunings were easier to use than "standard." They also provided different and exciting sounds, especially at the hands of talented blues guitarists.

Over the course of the 20th century, adventurous players have experimented greatly with the tunings of the open strings. As time progressed, many of the newer tunings no longer produced a vanilla major chord. But their advantages in other areas, easy access to particular scales and rich chords, far outweighed the loss of an open-string chord. Inventive players like England's Davey Graham and John Renbourn, pop stars Joni Mitchell and David Crosby, and Windham Hill guitar whiz Michael Hedges have stretched the boundaries of guitar tunings well past that of major and minor chords.

Tunings that don't necessarily produce a major chord with their open strings are commonly referred to as "alternate" tunings, as opposed to "open" tunings. In this book we will study both. For ease, we will include open-chord tunings under the heading of alternate tunings.

The Tunings In This Book

These first chapters in *The Complete Book of Alternate Tunings* provide the book's main substance. Included in each chapter are scales in the most commonly used keys for reach alternate tuning. Directly following the scales, you will find a "Waterfall" scale for each tuning. These exercises will introduce you to the art of juxtaposing open and fretted strings in a scalar passage to approximate the sustained sound of a harp. Each chapter also contains an abundance of usable chord fingerings for its tuning.

The book also provides descriptions of the tunings used in slide guitar playing, as well as a wealth of tunings used in the Hawaiian "Slack Key" style. There is even a chapter in the book on designing your own tunings.

The Artists' Listings

An additional wealth of material is contained in the Artists' Tunings section. This chapter includes tune and tuning listings from over 180 recorded artists. The source of each song title--whether it be an album, a book, or a magazine article--has been listed if it was at all possible to determine it.

Much of the material in the Artists' Listings came from well over two decades of work by the author: figuring out tunings from recordings, as well as working with many of the artists as a magazine editor and guitar music publisher. Most of the remainder of the material has come directly from the artists themselves.

Purposes of the Book

There are two main purposes for this book. The first is to provide you with an overview of many of the most common tunings in use today. I have attempted to provide you with a practical method of learning new tunings; by explaining who uses each tuning and why, and to show you how to produce each tuning from standard

The second reason for this book's existence is to provide you with as comprehensive a list as possible of the alternate tunings that 20th century guitarists use, and where you can find the tunings in use.

The Complete Book

With the preponderance of guitarists using alternate tunings in the modern guitar world, from some of the most famous rock groups to some of the most obscure folk singers, there is no way that a book like this could ever be "complete." As soon as the listings are ready for the printer, artists will have developed new tunings and new music using them. Perhaps we should have called the book the Almost Complete Book of Alternate Tunings or the Never Complete Book of Alternate Tunings! Complete or not, we think that you will be happy with the amount of material in the book, and the quality of the contents.

Consider this book a reference work. To learn all of the material contained in it is beyond even the most dedicated guitarist. Take it tuning by tuning. You may discover one particular tuning that suits you so well that you will find it unnecessary to use others. Others of you may want to use as many as possible.

However you pursue the information in this book, I hope that you have a great time using it. I suspect that you will use it for many years to come.

--Mark Hanson

Introduction

Before You Start Retuning

You must be aware before you venture into the land of alternate tunings that guitar strings have a tendency to break when retuned. They can break either as you tighten or loosen them. You must be careful. Flying strings can do damage to the human body. Face the guitar away from yourself, and anyone else around, as you retune.

If a string feels too tight as you approach a designated pitch, consider putting on a lighter gauge string. You could also tune the other strings down the appropriate amount so that you still produce the proper intervals between each pair of strings, but at a lower, less stressful pitch.

The tunings are written in letter names, from the bass string to the treble (from the sixth string to the first). Many publications print the letter names in upper case letters only. This can cause confusion, however, as to what octave the notes are in. We rectify that situation by using the conventional upper and lower case letters, with and without prime markings. The letter names themselves indicate not only the pitch of each string, but the octave as well. Here is how it works:

> a) Lower case with a prime (d´, e´) indicates Middle C and the octave above it (c´ to b´). Most often these pitches are located on the first string--occasionally on the second;
>
> b) Lower case without a prime (a, b) indicates the octave below Middle C (c to b). Most often these pitches are located on the second, third, and fourth strings;
>
> c) Upper case (E, A) indicates the second octave below Middle C (C to B). Most often these pitches are located on the fifth and sixth strings;
>
> d) Upper case with a prime (A´, B´) indicates the third octave below Middle C (C´ to B´). These pitches are quite low, and most often are located on the sixth string.

Chromatic Tuners

Consider buying a chromatic tuner. Unless you have absolute pitch, or very good relative pitch, an electronic tuner that registers chromatic notes will save you considerable effort.

I have never been a big fan of tuners, having learned to fine-tune a guitar before electronic tuners became widely available. But they certainly have their place, especially if you are retuning your guitar on a regular basis, or if you are a newcomer to this. A tuner may save you much frustration and many broken strings.

Standard Tuning

In each of the tuning chapters in this book I will present you with a number of items designed to help you most efficiently learn the tuning. After some initial insight into each tuning, I will explain how to get your guitar in tune for the tuning in that chapter. For easy reference, I will provide a chart, depicting five items:

1) the string numbers (6 is the bass string, 1 is the treble);
2) the pitches of standard tuning;
3) the pitches of the new tuning;
4) which strings must change--and by how much--to produce the new tuning from standard; and,
5) --to make sure that you have the new tuning in tune--the frets you finger on each string to match the pitch of the adjacent open (unfretted) string. The chart on this page compares standard and drop-D tunings, even though we won't cover DropD until the next chapter.

Strings	Standard	Drop-D	Change(s)	Fret to Match Adjacent Open String
1	e´	e´	--	--
2	b	b	--	5
3	g	g	--	4
4	d	d	--	5
5	A	A	--	5
6	E	D	Lower 1 whole-step	7

Why Start With Standard Tuning?

We will start with standard tuning for a variety of reasons. First and foremost, it is the most common tuning, and, in many respects, the most flexible. It allows for relatively easy access to music in the full range of keys, as well as atonal music, if you are so inclined. Also, starting with standard tuning allows you to work through the format of the chapters using very familiar fingerings.

I have provided scale material in standard notation and tablature in several positions on the neck. These scales are in the five most common guitar keys, C, A, G, E and D. The three sets of ascending scales are followed by a descending "waterfall" scale. This scale introduces you to the art of juxtaposing fretted and open strings within a scale passage. With some practice on these cascading scales, you can begin to imitate the sustained sound of a harp.

An assortment of usable chord fingerings for the tuning follows the scale exercises. The chords are organized according to the key of the scale that precedes them. I have done my best to diagram chord voicings that you will enjoy, are relatively easy to play, and expand a bit beyond the standard major or minor triad. Once we get into some of the altered tunings, you will find that quite simple fingerings can provide exceedingly rich chord voicings. This is one of the most enjoyable aspects of working with alternate tunings.

At the end of a number of the chapters, I supply a list of tunings that are close to the featured tuning. Mostly these neighboring tunings require only one string to be altered from the main tuning. In addition, you will get a list of recorded tunes that use the featured tuning. Now, let's get started!

Getting in Tune

Standard tuning, E A d g b e´, is tuned mostly in intervals of perfect fourths. A perfect fourth is the distance from the first note to the fourth note of a *do-re-mi* scale, from *do* to *fa*, if you like. You can memorize this interval by relating it to the first interval of the melody of "Here Comes the Bride." The first two notes of "Columbia, the Gem of the Ocean" also comprise a perfect fourth interval. If you play two adjacent open strings in standard tuning with the rhythm of the melody of "Here Comes the Bride," it should sound like that song if the strings are in tune.

There is one exception to this rule: the distance between the second and third strings in standard tuning is a major third interval. You can recognize a major third interval as the "Da-Da-Da-Dum" melody from Beethoven's Fifth Symphony.

First, use your fifth-fret tuning technique to tune your guitar (i.e. the fifth fret of a string is the same pitch as the adjacent higher-pitched string, unfretted). Of course, the one exception to the fifth-fret rule is the third string, where you fret the fourth fret to match the open second string.

Another way to get in tune is to check octaves and unisons. If you have ever watched piano tuners work, you will have noticed that they tune the octaves and unisons exactly in tune. (Many of the strings on the piano are doubled and even tripled. If these unisons are not in tune, you get the honky-tonk piano effect!) You should attempt their octave tuning method on the guitar as well.

The following tuning chart suggests where to fret the strings to fine-tune your instrument using both unisons and octaves. Remember, you can always go back to your electronic tuner for help!

Unison and Octave Tuning Chart--Standard Tuning

Scales in Standard Tuning

In each tunings chapter I will provide scales in the keys that work well in that particular tuning. In standard tuning, the most common guitar keys are C, G, D, A and E. The following music examples provide scales in each area of the neck. Practice each scale until you are comfortable with the spacings and the fingerings. Be aware that the tablature provides all of the locations on each string up to the twelfth fret.

Then, for fun, I have provided a cascading "waterfall" scale for each key. The idea here is to imitate the sustained sound of a harp. Let each note of the passage ring as long as possible as you pick the succeeding notes. There will be moments when three consecutive scale notes will be ringing simultaneously on three different strings! This likely will give your fretting hand a workout if you aren't accustomed to this type of exercise.

Have fun with these!

C Major Scale in Three Positions--Standard Tuning

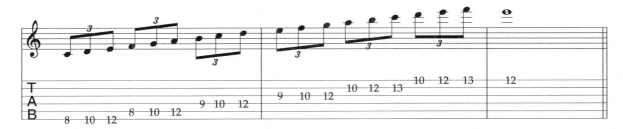

C Major "Waterfall" Scale--Standard Tuning

G Major Scale in Three Positions--Standard Tuning

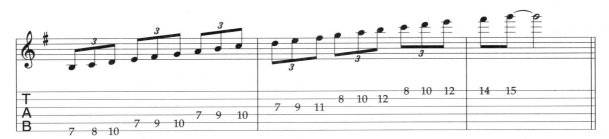

G Major "Waterfall" Scale--Standard Tuning

D Major Scale in Three Positions--Standard Tuning

D Major "Waterfall" Scale--Standard Tuning

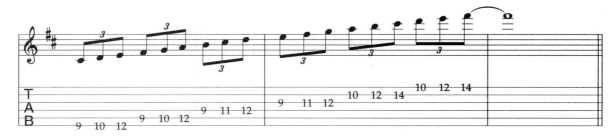

A Major Scale in Three Positions--Standard Tuning

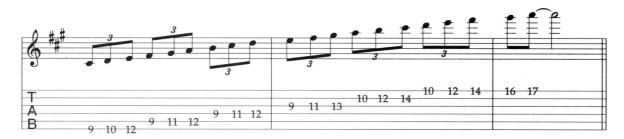

A Major "Waterfall" Scale--Standard Tuning

E Major Scale in Three Positions--Standard Tuning

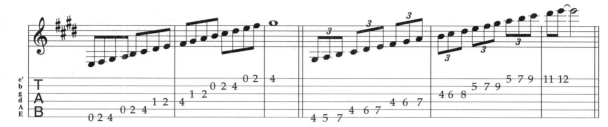

E Major "Waterfall" Scale--Standard Tuning

A Minor Scale in Three Positions--Standard Tuning

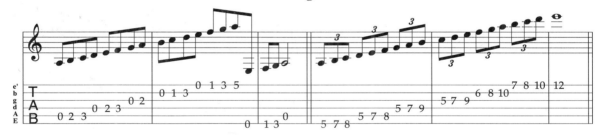

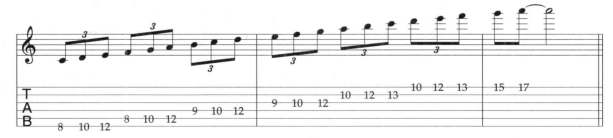

A Minor "Waterfall" Scale--Standard Tuning

E Minor Scale in Three Positions--Standard Tuning

E Minor "Waterfall" Scale--Standard Tuning

D Minor Scale in Three Positions--Standard Tuning

D Minor "Waterfall" Scale--Standard Tuning

Chord Fingerings

I have diagrammed a number of chord fingerings for you to use in each tuning. There are many fingerings and voicings for every chord, and I have not attempted to be exhaustive. Rather, I have tried to provide a good sampling of fingerings that you may wish to try.

Key of C Chords

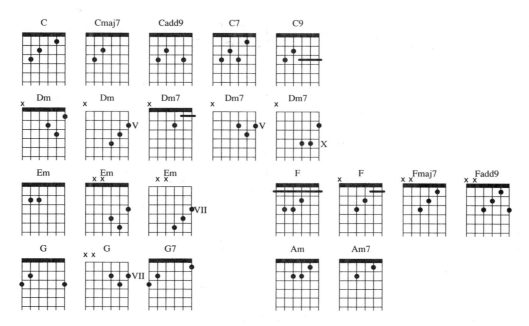

Key of G Chords

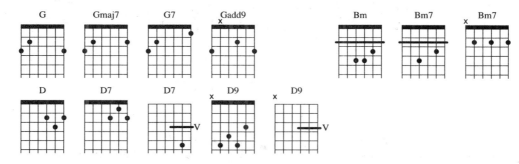

Key of D Chords

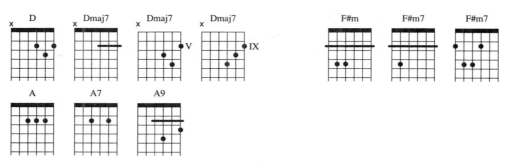

Key of A Chords

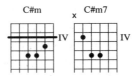

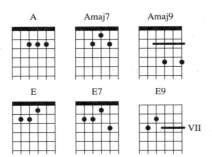

Key of E Chords

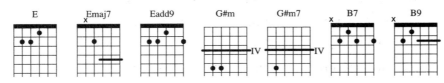

Key of A Minor Chords

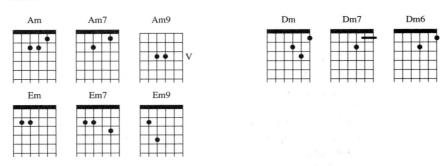

Key of E Minor Chords

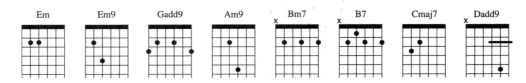

Key of D Minor Chords

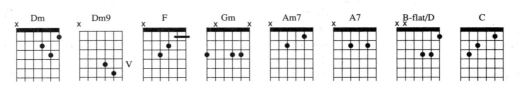

Chords Grouped By Keys

Many chords overlap from key to key. I have made a minimum of effort to duplicate all of these chord diagrams from one key to the next on the preceding pages. Rather, I will provide you with the following list of diatonic chords in each key, so that you can make an effort to memorize the chords that generally are used together. You can then find the appropriate fingerings amongst the chord diagrams.

Key of C:	C, Dm, Em, F, G (G7), Am
Key of G:	G, Am, Bm, C, D (D7), Em
Key of D:	D Em, F#m, G, A (A7), Bm
Key of A:	A, Bm, C#m, D, E (E7), F#m
Key of E:	E, F#m, G#m, A, B (B7), C#m
Key of A minor:	Am, C, Dm, Em (E7), F, G
Key of E minor:	Em, G, Am, Bm (B7), C, D
Key of D minor:	Dm, F Gm , Am (A7), B^b, C

Standard Tuning Recordings

Artist	Tune	Source
Beatles	"Blackbird"	White Album
Blind Blake	"Diddie Wa Diddie"	Search Warrant Blues, Vol. 2
Eric Clapton	"Tears In Heaven"	Unplugged
Crosby, Stills & Nash	"Helplessly Hoping"	Crosby, Stills & Nash
John Denver	"Take Me Home, Country Roads"	Greatest Hits, Vol. 1
Donovan	"Jennifer, Juniper"	Greatest Hits
Fleetwood Mac	"Landslide"	Fleetwood Mac
	"Oh, Well"	Then Play On
Dan Fogelberg	"Leader of the Band"	Greatest Hits
Grateful Dead	"Friend of the Devil"	American Beauty
Arlo Guthrie	"Alice's Restaurant"	Alice's Restaurant
Heart	"Crazy On You"	Dreamboat Annie
Kansas	"Dust in the Wind"	Point of Know Return
Leo Kottke	"William Powell"	My Father's Face
	"Twilight Time"	Peculiaroso
Led Zeppelin	"Stairway to Heaven"	Led Zeppelin IV
	"Babe, I'm Gonna Leave You"	Led Zeppelin I
Don McLean	"American Pie"	American Pie
Ralph McTell	"Streets of London"	Streets of London
Police	"Every Breath You Take"	Synchonicity
Paul Simon	"Sounds of Silence"	Sounds of Silence
	"Anji"	Sounds of Silence
Bruce Springsteen	"I'm On Fire"	Born in the U.S.A.
James Taylor	"Fire and Rain"	Sweet Baby James
Merle Travis	"John Henry"	The Best of Merle Travis
Edward Van Halen	"Spanish Fly"	Van Halen 2
Dave Van Ronk	"Cocaine Blues"	Dave Van Ronk, Folk Singer
Traffic	"John Barleycorn"	John Barleycorn
Mason Williams	"Classical Gas"	Phonograph Record
Neil Young	"Needle and the Damage Done"	Harvest

Drop D Tuning

D A d g b e'

If you haven't worked with alternate tunings in the past, Drop D is the place to start. The only difference from standard tuning is that the bass string is tuned down one whole-step to a D.

As you might expect, the low D note adds an abundance of richness to a D chord. Consequently, most tunes that use Drop D tuning are in the key of D. However, Drop D works well in the keys of G and A as well.

If you are familiar with standard tuning, you will find Drop D quite easy to use. The tuning does not affect any of the scale or chord fingerings on the five treble strings. To play the same notes as standard tuning, the fingerings on the bass string move up two frets.

Drop D tuning is a favorite among fingerstyle players. Virtuosos Ry Cooder and Leo Kottke use the tuning extensively. Pop singers like James Taylor and John Denver have recorded tunes that use it. And the late fingerstylist Joseph Spence from the Bahamas used Drop D tuning exclusively.

You will also find Drop D used by rock bands like Pearl Jam ("Garden"), the Beatles ("Dear Prudence"), and The Band ("Jemima Surrender"). Blues duo Hot Tuna, featuring one-time Jefferson Airplane guitarist Jorma Kaukonen, is famous for his Drop D guitar instrumental "Embryonic Journey." Stephen Still's solo tune "Treetop Flyer" also uses Drop D tuning.

Even guitarists who avoid alternate tunings in general--classical guitarists, for instance--will use Drop D. Much of the soundtrack work that Laurindo Almeida has done over the years has used Drop D. And the stunning solo guitar arrangements of the music of Antonio Carlos Jobim by Carlos Barbosa-Lima use Drop D tuning. Let's go to it!

Tuning to Drop D

Lower your bass string one whole-step to D. Steel-string guitars will need about a one-third turn of the tuning peg. Nylon-string guitars will likely need somewhat more than that. The pitch of the seventh-fret note on the bass string should now equal the open fifth string. The rest of the strings are tuned like standard tuning. The following diagrams show the tuning and how to check for good intonation, using unisons and octaves.

Strings	Standard	Drop-D	Change(s)	Fret to Match Adjacent Open String
1	e´	e´	--	--
2	b	b	--	5
3	g	g	--	4
4	d	d	--	5
5	A	A	--	5
6	E	D	Lower 1 whole-step	7

Unison and Octave Tuning Chart--Drop-D Tuning

Scales in Drop D

As I mentioned earlier, Drop D tuning can be used in a variety of keys. D major is the most common, simply because the root note of the tonic chord--D--is in the bass. That provides a beautifully rich, root-position (D-in-the-bass) tonic chord (D major) for the key. The same is true of D minor, although that key is a little less common than D major.

The key of G works very well in Drop D tuning. That low D bass note is now the root note of the dominant chord of the key--the chord built on the fifth note of a G scale: namely, a D! The dominant chord is most western harmonic systems is the second most important chord in the key, after the tonic chord (the chord built on the first note of the scale).

The key of A is the other key that we will cover in this tuning. In the key of A, a D note is the fourth note of the scale. That makes the rich D chord with the low sixth string on the bottom the subdominant chord in the key of A-- the third most important chord.

The following scales will show you around Drop D in the keys of D major and minor, G Major and A major.

D Major Scale in Three Positions--Drop-D

D Major "Waterfall"Scale--Drop-D

D Minor Scale in Three Positions--Drop-D

D Minor "Waterfall" Scale--Drop-D

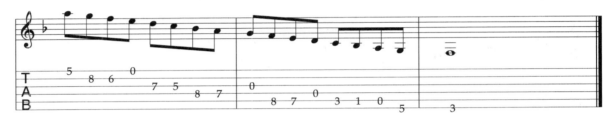

G Major Scale in Three Positions--Drop D Tuning

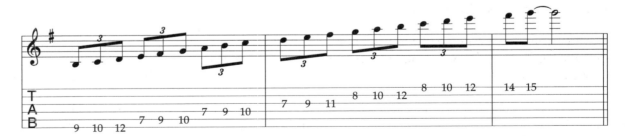

G Major "Waterfall" Scale--Drop-D

A Major Scale in Three Positions--Drop D

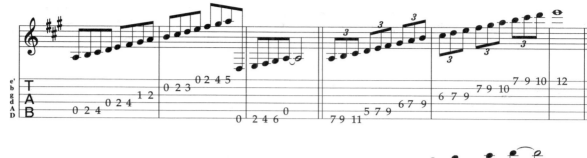

A Major "Waterfall" Scale--Drop-D

Chord Fingerings

Drop D tuning provides all kinds of possibilities for beautifully rich D major and minor chords. I have shown many in the accompanying fretboard diagrams.

As you work with these fingerings, begin to train your ear to pick out the root note of each chord (the note the chord is built on; C in a C chord, for instance). As you develop your ability to pick out the root, then start listening for the third and the fifth in the chords as well. In a D chord, for instance, the root is the D, the third is an F#, and the fifth is an A. The three notes of a G chord are G, B and D--root, third, and fifth. An A chord consists of A, C#, and E.

Eventually, as you develop your ability to pick out each of those notes in your chord fingerings, you will be able to determine how to alter each fingering to produce more complex harmonies. Chords that may have sounded exotic to you in the past--like major and minor 7ths, 9ths, 11ths, 13ths, and suspensions-- will become familiar friends.

We will discuss this more in upcoming chapters. For now, spend some time learning these fingerings. Experiment putting different fingerings together in a pattern. For instance, try a simple D-G-A7-D first. Then try Dadd9-Bm7-Em11-A9sus. You may find these chord progressions and the "voicings" that you use to produce them will suggest new compositions.

Chords in Drop D

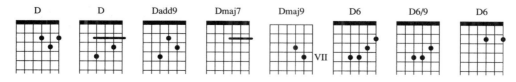

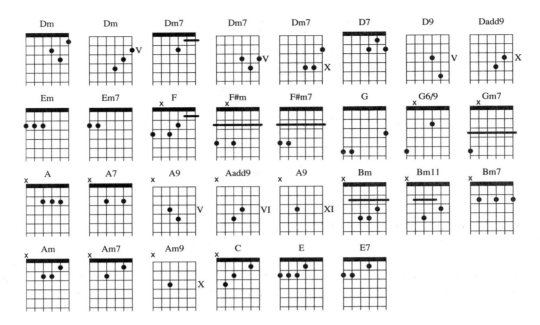

Drop D Tuning Recordings

Artist	Tune	Source
Chet Atkins	All Thumbs	Me and My Guitar
Carlos Barbosa-Lima	Corcovado	Barbosa-Lima Plays the Music of Jobim & Gershwin
Bruce Cockburn	God Bless the Children	Night Vision
Ry Cooder	FDR in Trinidad	Into the Purple Valley
David Crosby	Carry Me	Wind on the Water
Peppino D'Agostino	Bossa for Francesca	Sparks
Alex deGrassi	Children's Dance	Turning: Turning Back
John Denver	Rocky Mountain High	Greatest Hits
Doyle Dykes	Amazing Grace	Fingerstyle Guitar
Rick Emmett	Midsummer's Dream	Stages (Triumph)
Nanci Griffith	Lone Star State of Mind	Lone Star State of Mind
Mark Hanson	Boogie Woogie Jingle Bells	Yuletide Guitar
Janis Ian	This Train Still Runs	Breaking Silence
Bert Jansch	Ramblin's Gonna Be the Death of Me	Lucky 13
Jorma Kaukonen	Embryonic Journey	Magic
John Knowles	Vincent	Fingerstyle Quarterly
Leo Kottke	Mona Ray	Dreams and All That Stuff
Adrian Legg	Anu	Guitar for Mortals
Don McLean	Castles in the Air	Tapestry
Pearl Jam	Garden	Ten
Ken Perlman	Fisher's Hornpipe	Fingerpicking Fiddle Tunes
Al Pettaway	Festival Waltz	Whispering Stones
Chris Proctor	Fond Farewells	His Journey Home
Preston Reed	Accufuse	Playing By Ear
Harvey Reid	Annie Laurie	Chestnuts
John Renbourn	Lady Goes to Church	Sir John Alot
Breve Reussner	Anecdota	Song Without Words
Pete Seeger	Living in the Country	Greatest Hits
Martin Simpson	Banks of the Bann	Leaves of Life
Doug Smith	When the Walls Fell	Labyrinth
Joseph Spence	Glory, Glory	Folk Guitar
James Taylor	Country Road	Sweet Baby James
Richard Thompson	Beeswing	Mirror Blue
Happy Traum	Worried Blues	Bucket of Blues
Guy Van Duser	Guitar Boogie Shuffle	Finger-Style Guitar Solos
Dave Van Ronk	Sunday Street	Sunday Street
David Wilcox	All the Roots Grow Deeper	Big Horizon

Double Drop D

D A d g b d'

This is a wonderful tuning. It has several names, including "Double Drop D" and Double D Down." It is identical to Drop D tuning, except that the first string is also lowered one whole-step to D.

This was a popular tuning among Buffalo Springfield members from the '60s: Neil Young and Stephen Stills. Since then it has become quite popular among fingerstyle soloists like John Renbourn, Adrian Legg, Chris Proctor, and Ed Gerhard.

Stephen Stills' acoustic guitar solo on his song "Bluebird" from Buffalo Springfield Again initially introduced me to this tuning. As I listened to the record (still used vinyl in those days!), I could tell that Stills was a Drop D tuning of sorts. But he played a chord at the end of the instrumental section that was simply impossible in Drop D, a Cmaj9 with a D note as the highest pitch on the first string. After tuning the first string down to D, I was able to recreate his chord.

Stills went on to use this tuning on a number of songs: notably "Black Queen" from his first solo album, and "Find the Cost of Freedom" (lowered one whole-step to C G c f a c´) from the Crosby, Stills, Nash & Young album So Far. Neil Young has used this tuning extensively as well. His CSN&Y hit "Ohio" lies nicely in D A d g b d´, as does "Cinnamon Girl" from his first solo album.

More recently, John Renbourn has used D A d g b d´ to set a lovely version of the Celtic tune "Southwind." A tune from famed Irish harper and composer Turlough O'Carolan, "Si Bhig, Si Mhor" was set beautifully in this tuning by Ed Gerhard. And Adrian Legg and Chris Proctor have composed extensively in D A d g b d´.

Getting in Tune in D A d g b d'

Lower your bass string one whole-step like Drop D. Then lower the first string one whole-step as well. You should now have three D strings: the sixth, fourth, and first. The third-fret note on the second string should equal the open first string.

Here are the diagrams to help you fine-tune D A d g b d´.

Strings	Standard	DAdgbd´	Change(s)	Fret to Match Adjacent Open String
1	e´	d´	Lower 1 whole-step	--
2	b	b	--	3
3	g	g	--	4
4	d	d	--	5
5	A	A	--	5
6	E	D	Lower 1 whole-step	7

Unison and Octave Tuning Chart--D A d g b d´

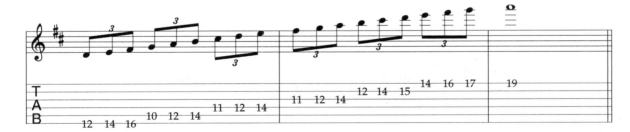

Scales in DAdgbd'

Mostly players use the key of D in D A d g b d´, but I have also diagrammed D minor and G major scales for you. The open strings of the tuning nearly produce a G chord--only the open fifth string is not a member of a G triad. So the key of G works quite well.

Realize that these scale positions are almost the same as standard and Drop D. The inner four strings (the second, third, fourth, and fifth) are the same as they are in standard tuning, so the positions of notes on those strings will not change. The scale notes of the first and sixth string are raised two frets because of the retuning.

D Major Scale in Three Positions--D A d g b d'

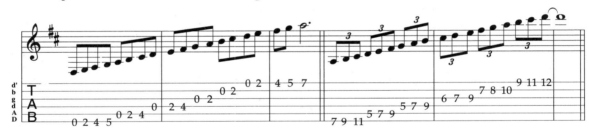

D Major "Waterfall" Scale--D A d g b d'

D Minor Scale in Three Positions--D A d g b d'

D Minor "Waterfall" Scale--D A d g b d'

G Major (D Blues) Scale in Three Positions--D A d g b d'

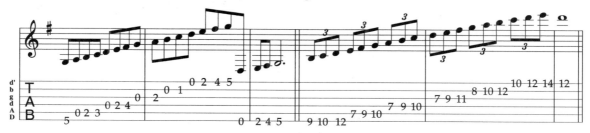

G Major (D Blues) "Waterfall" Scale--D A d g b d'

Chords in D A d g b d'

In D A d g b d′ tuning, the four inner strings of the guitar are still in standard tuning. As you practice the chords diagrammed here, visualize your standard tuning chords for those strings. The notes on the first and sixth strings are simply up two frets from their positions in standard tuning.

You will find the open first-string d′ to be a very useful note. In a first-position D chord, it can match the pitch of the third fret of the second string, producing a 12-string effect of unison treble notes. It can make a D fingering exceedingly easy.

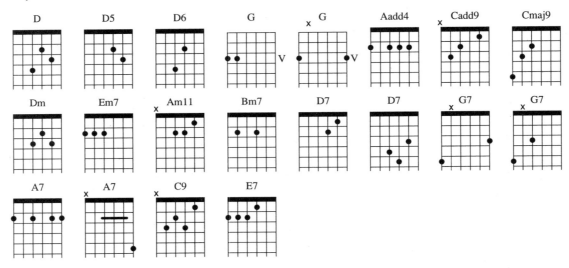

The open first string d′ is also very useful in G chords and A chords. Since a D note is part of a G chord, it is not necessary to fret the first string to produce a G chord sound. The open second, third, and fourth strings in this tuning (and in standard), are the three notes of a G chord already. With that in mind, you may fret the two outside strings together at the fifth, ninth, or twelfth frets and produce G chords. For these fingerings, you need to omit the fifth string from your strum or picking pattern by muting it, or, simply avoid striking it.

In the case of an A chord, the first-string d′ provides the suspended fourth of the chord. This note is beautiful juxtaposed with the second-fret, second-string note in an A major chord. And it is particularly beautiful juxtaposed with the first-fret, second string note in the case of an A minor chord. This chord is an Am11, a minor chord that has both the third and the fourth notes of an A scale in it. Lovely! Make up some chord fingerings of your own!

Recordings in D A d g b d'

Artist	Tune	Source
Peter Finger	Petermann's Polka	Acoustic Rock Guitar
Ed Gerhard	Si Bhig, Si Mhor	Night Birds
Mark Hanson	Strawberry Curl	Art of Solo Fingerpicking
Adrian Legg	Nail Talk	Guitars & Other Cathedrals
	Tracy's Big Moment	Guitars & Other Cathedrals
Chris Proctor	Canyonlands	Runoff
	Desert Dance	His Journey Home
	Hewlett	Steel String Stories
Stephen Stills	Black Queen	Stephen Stills
	Find the Cost of Freedom	So Far (CSN&Y)
	Bluebird	Buffalo Springfield Again
Neil Young	Cinnamon Girl	Neil Young
	Ohio	So Far (CSN&Y)
	When You Dance I Can Really Love	After the Goldrush

D sus 4
D A d g a d'

This tuning is a favorite of Celtic players. It does not contain the third of a D chord (f#), so it implies neither a major nor minor modality. It is a perfect tuning for playing many of the modal traditional melodies of the British Isles, with an underlying drone accompaniment of open strings.

D A d g a d' (commonly pronounced "Dad Gad") was developed by English guitarist Davey Graham as he attempted to play with the oud players of Morocco around 1960. He brought it back to England, where leading fingerstylists like John Renbourn and Bert Jansch used it for their own compositions, as well as for the accompaniment of traditional singers. Even famed rocker Jimmy Page used the tuning for his well-known acoustic instrumental "Black Mountain Side" from Led Zeppelin I. (Earlier, Jansch had developed a similar guitar arrangement in Drop D tuning for his accompaniment of the traditional tune "Blackwaterside.")

The tuning has become the "standard" tuning of gifted French fingerstylist Pierre Bensusan. His understanding of the tuning is as thorough as any virtuoso's understanding of standard tuning. Pierre has gone so far as to name his promotional company DADGAD Music!

The Intervals of D A d g a d'

This is the first tuning that we have encountered that includes a very small interval (the distance between two notes) between open strings: a major second. This interval consists of one whole-step, the distance of two frets on the guitar neck. On the piano, this is the distance from one white note to the next, if there is a black note between them. All of the other intervals between strings in D A d g a d' are perfect fourths, the same as in standard.

Having a major second interval between strings opens up all kinds of interesting possibilities for the guitarist. You can now play consecutive scale notes without having to fret either of the notes. That is something you can't do in standard tuning. Or, you can play consecutive scale notes with a simple barre fingering over the two strings. This will come in very handy when you begin working at imitating the sustained sound of a harp in the Celtic style.

In the key of D, D A d g a d' tuning has the suspended fourth (g) of a D chord as the open third string. All the rest of the open strings are either the root note (D) or the fifth (A) of a D chord. Since the third of a chord is the note that defines whether the chord is major or minor, the open strings of D A d g a d' are neither. You need an f or an f# on the open third string to produce a major or minor chord with the open strings. (We'll get to that in subsequent chapters!)

To the average listener's ear, a suspended fourth chord generally wants to resolve somewhere--to move to another chord that is a bit more stable or final sounding. Building this feeling of anticipation right into the tuning is a wonderful concept. Knowledgeable composers certainly consider the effect of certain chords as they compose. You might be aware of this concerning what tunings you use, as well.

Getting in Tune in D A d g a d'

From standard tuning, lower the two outside strings (sixth and first) one whole-step to D. Also, lower the second string one whole-step from b to a. The second fret of the third string should now equal the open second string.

The accompanying charts depict the tuning for D A d g a d' as compared to standard. Make sure that you understand the "Fret to Match Adjacent Open String" column in the tuning chart. It simply means that to match pitches between two strings, you fret the lower-pitched string at the designated fret, while playing the adjacent higher-pitched string *unfretted*. Once those strings are in tune, you will use the next fret number from the column to tune the next pair of strings.

Strings	Standard	DAdgad'	Change(s)	Fret to Match Adjacent Open String
1	e'	d'	Lower 1 whole-step	--
2	b	a	Lower 1 whole step	5
3	g	g	--	2
4	d	d	--	5
5	A	A	--	5
6	E	D	Lower 1 whole-step	7

Unison and Octave Tuning Chart--D A D g a d'

Scales

D A d g a d' is used mostly to play in the key of D. I have included both D major and D minor scales for you, since you likely will come across pieces in both modalities. I have also included G major, since this tuning can work nicely in that key as well. One reason all of these keys work so well in this tuning is that all of the notes of the open strings--D, A, and G--are included in all three keys.

If you have trouble with the shifting positions of these scale notes (as compare to standard tuning), try thinking of them this way: the third-, fourth-, and fifth-string notes are all in the same places as standard tuning. So none of the scale or chord fingerings is altered on those strings.

The two treble strings are the same distance from each other as they are in standard tuning (a "perfect fourth" interval--five half-steps). That means that you can play scales and two-note chords on the two treble strings as if they were in standard tuning. You simply have to fret the notes on those strings two frets higher than you would in standard tuning to match the rest of the strings in D A d g a d'.

Treat the lowered bass string the same as Drop D tuning.

D Major Scale in Three Positions--D A d g a d'

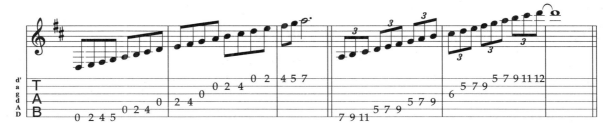

D Major "Waterfall" Scale--D A d g a d'

D Minor Scales in Three Positions--D A d g a d´

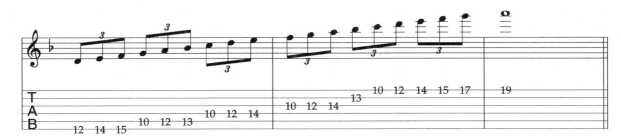

D Minor "Waterfall" Scale--D A d g a d'

G Major Scales in Three Positions--D A d g a d´

G Major "Waterfall" Scale--D A d g a d'

Chords in D A d g a d'

The proximity of the pitches of the second and third strings in D A d g a d´ not only provides satisfying melodic juxtapositions, but lovely harmonies as well. Since western harmony is based on intervals of a third, introducing seconds into the chords can have a striking effect on the ear.

Very commonly, the second, fourth, sixth and seventh notes of a scale are added to a basic major or minor chord (consisting of the first, third and fifth notes of the scale) to produce a richer harmonies. These added notes are no more than an interval of a second (a half-step or whole-step) away from one of the notes of the basic triad. Sometimes these extra notes are raised or lowered a half-step from where they lie in the normal scale.

How these notes are combined with the basic major or minor triad can help determine a style. For instance, characteristic chords in swing music contain the sixth of the scale, in addition to the normal triad. The blues normally adds the seventh note (lowered one half-step) of the scale to a major triad. Celtic music often adds the ninth and the fourth of the scale, often with notes allowed to sustain into the next chord, in the manner of a harp.

Many of the following D A d g a d´ chord voicings introduce notes other than the normal root, third, and fifth of a major or minor chord. Experiment with these voicings, and try inventing some of your own!

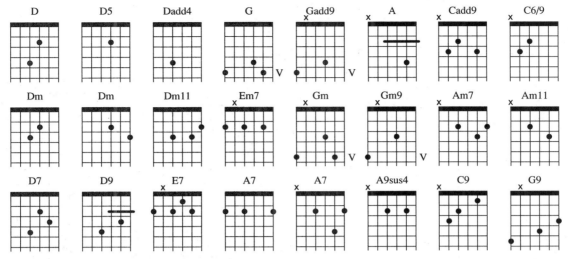

Recordings in DAdgad'

Artist	Tune	Source
William Ackerman	The Moment	Imaginary Roads
Pierre Bensusan	Around the Day in 80 Worlds	Wu Wei
Peppino D'Agostino	Beyond the Dunes	Close to the Heart
Alex deGrassi	Mirage	Collection
Doyle Dykes	The Great Roundup	Fingerstyle Guitar
Peter Finger	Sinn Ohne Wörte	Inner Life
Ed Gerhard	Tennessee	Luna
Nanci Griffith	Ghost in the Music	Blue Moon
Stefan Grossman	Woman From Donori	Snap a Little Owl
Mark Hanson	Twin Sisters	Art of Solo Fingerpicking
Michael Hedges	Ragamuffin	Aerial Boundaries
Bert Jansch	St. Fiacre	A Rare Conundrum
Laurence Juber	Pass the Buck	LJ
Phil Keaggy	County Down	Acoustic Solos
Pat Kirtley	Blind Mary	Irish Guitar
Adrian Legg	Coging's Glory	Guitar for Mortals
Dougie MacLean	Little Ones Walk On	Whitewash
Bill Mize	Sugarlands	Sugarlands
Jimmy Page	Black Mountain Side	Led Zeppelin I
Al Pettaway	Amy's Tears	Midsummer Moon
John Renbourn	A Maid That's Deep In Love	A Maid That's Deep In Love
Eric Schoenberg	Rights of Man	Steel Strings
Martin Simpson	The Turtle and the Asp	Red Roses
Doug Smith	Renewal	Order of Magnitude
David Surette	The Month of January	Fingerstyle Guitar Magazine #8
Richard Thompson	Two Left Feet	Hand of Kindness
David Wilcox	Strong Chemistry	Big Horizon

Related Tunings

Michael Hedges B´A d g a d´	Funky Avocado	Breakfast in the Field
Martin Simpson D A d g a c´	Lucy Wan	Leaves of Life

Open D
D A d f# a d'

Open D tuning is not only one of the best sounding tunings, it also is one of the easiest to play.

This amazingly rich tuning is so powerful because of the voicing of the open strings. The root note of the normal tonic chord in this tuning, namely D, is the lowest pitch in the bass. This is called a "root position" chord, a stronger sounding chord than of any of the inversions. (Inversions are chords with a note other than the root as the lowest bass note).

This tuning also has the root note on the top. The close voicing in the upper range (four notes all within one octave) and the open-fifth interval between the two bass strings (a very strong voicing) make this a perfectly voiced chord to project strength and finality.

Open D has been a mainstay in the library of tunings for well over a century. The tuning was used in a quite famous 19th century piece entitled "Sebastopol." It, along with an Open G tuning piece called "Spanish Fandango," became quite popular during the parlor guitar era of the 1800s.

By the early 1900s, Open D tuning had become known by the title of the earlier composition, "Sebastopol" or "Vestapol." Vestapol tuning gained widespread popularity among bluesmen playing slide guitar at that time. The tuning was exceedingly easy to use: chords could be made without fretting the strings at all, or by fretting with one finger. Plus, being able to produce full major chords by holding a slide straight across the strings was particularly attractive to blues players. With the slide, they could effectively imitate the scooping and moaning of a blues singer, and simultaneously complete the chordal accompaniment on the other strings.

The popularity of Open D tuning continues to this day, but not only among slide guitar players. You will find Open D tuning and its many variants (among them: open D minor, D A d f a d´; Open D major7, D A d f# a c#´; and Open D7, D A d f# a c´) used by blues and slide players (Ry Cooder, John Lee Hooker, George Thorogood, Chris Whitley), folk singers (Joni Mitchell, Richie Havens), contemporary fingerstylists (Leo Kottke, Alex deGrassi, William Ackerman, John Fahey, Martin Simpson), and rock bands (Nirvana, Pearl Jam, Allman Brothers, Eagles).

Getting In Tune In Open D

To produce open D tuning from standard, you follow the same procedure as producing D A d g a d´. Lower the first, second, and sixth strings one whole-step. Then go a step further: lower the third string one half-step to f#.

Strum the open strings. Hopefully they sound like a major chord. If not, tune it again, this time matching unisons: the seventh fret of the bass string equals the open fifth string; the fifth fret of the fifth string equals the open fourth; the fourth fret of the fourth string equals the open third; the third fret of the third string equals the open second; and the fifth fret of the second strings equals the open first string.

Try committing these fret positions to memory. It is easy to remember which frets you use on several strings, since they simply match the number of the string: third fret/third string; fourth fret/fourth string; fifth fret/fifth string. The bass string uses the seventh fret, which is the same as drop-D tuning. The first and second strings are the same

distance (a perfect fourth) from each other as they are in standard tuning. So you use the fifth fret of the second string to match the open first. Use the following chart to change your tuning to Open D.

Strings	Standard	DAdf#ad′	Change(s)	Fret to Match Adjacent Open String
1	e′	d′	Lower 1 whole-step	--
2	b	a	Lower 1 whole-step	5
3	g	f#	Lower 1 half-step	3
4	d	d	--	4
5	A	A	--	5
6	E	D	Lower 1 whole-step	7

Getting chord tunings like open D exactly in tune can be frustrating. The frustration lies in fine tuning the strings well enough that the chords actually sound in tune.

Assuming that you have a good quality guitar with relatively new strings, the trick to getting alternate tunings nicely in tune is making sure that the octaves and unisons match perfectly. Here is one method of fine tuning open D tuning: Fret the fifth and second strings at the fifth fret. Working in pairs, pick all of the strings except the third (the F#). All five of these notes are D, in three different octaves. They should all ring nicely together. Once those are in tune, fret the third string at the eighth fret. Does that pitch equal the open first string? It should.

Likely, at first you will have some trouble fine-tuning the guitar in an open tuning. Don't despair. I have seen some of the biggest names in the acoustic guitar world struggle to tune their guitars onstage, or play with the guitar less than perfectly in tune. It happens to everyone.

Open E tuning (E B e g# b e′, low to high), another variant of open D, has the same relationships string to string as open D, but is tuned one whole-step higher. This puts additional stress on the guitar (three strings are tuned higher than standard), and produces a brighter sound. But it may not be advisable for your particular instrument. If you need to play in open E, consider tuning to open D and placing a capo at the second fret.

Unison and Octave Tuning Chart--Open D (D A d f# a d′)

Scales

Because of its relatively limited fretting requirements, open D major can be among the simplest tunings to use on the guitar.

The advantages of playing in open D tuning are many. The usual tonic chord, D major, is played by simply

strumming the open strings. Other useful chords can be played by simply adding one or two fingers, or by fretting a simple barre. Melodies can be fretted on a single string, while harmony notes are provided by open strings.

The drawbacks, as in all altered tunings, are that the chord and scale positions are different from what you may be accustomed in standard tuning. Plus, in an open tuning it may not always be as easy to play in keys other than the key of the tuning--D major in the case of open D tuning.

Note: If you are a recreational player, I would suggest that you not spend too much time working on the scales located up the neck. For you, the beauty of this tuning likely will be in the chords you can produce, rather than the scales.

D Major Scale in Three Positions--D A d f# a d´

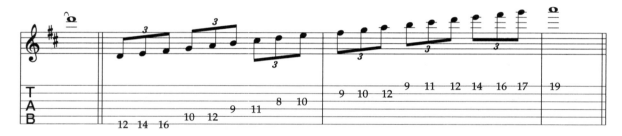

D Major "Waterfall" Scale--D A d f# a d'

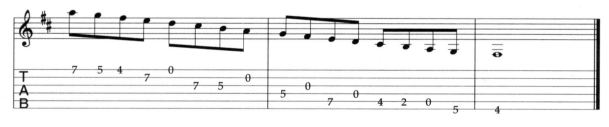

A Major Scale in Three Positions--D A d f# a d'

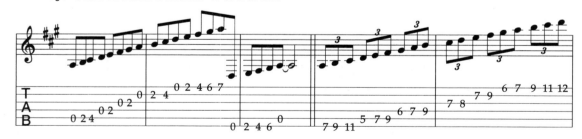

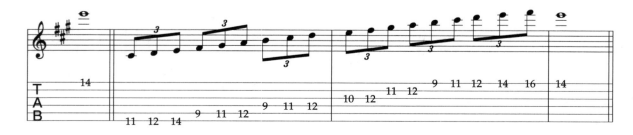

A Major "Waterfall" Scale--D A d f# a d'

Chords in D A d f# a d'

One of the main attractions of playing in most open tunings is the beautiful chords you can produce without too much effort on the part of your fretting hand. Playing simple major and minor chords is easy in most open-chord tunings, but adding some other notes to your basic chords can make open tunings sound especially rich.

A quick music theory lesson for you is in order here, so that you understand chord structure a bit. As I stated in an earlier chapter, major or minor chord consists of three notes: the first, third, and fifth notes of a major or minor scale (**do**-re-**mi**-fa-**sol**-la-ti). If you play those three notes together, *voila!* You have a chord. (A six-string major or minor chord on the guitar really has only three notes, which are doubled or tripled at different octaves.)

Adding other notes of the scale (re, fa, la, and ti) to those three can make the major and minor chords even richer sounding. This is where open tunings really shine.

In open D tuning, the open strings already provide the do, mi, and sol of a D-major chord. To add other notes (sixths, sevenths, ninths and elevenths) to this D chord, all you need to do is fret a note or two (or five!) somewhere on the neck.

I have diagrammed numerous chord fingerings that work beautifully in this tuning. Many have notes added to the one-three-five; some have even deleted one or more of those three!

Make up some chord progressions--like Em-A-D, or Em-F#m-G-A-Bm--and experiment with some of the different voicings diagrammed for each chord. Which voicings move smoothly from one to another? Which don't? Paying attention to what sounds good in your experiments will be a valuable lesson in voice leading for you.

As you develop your composing skills, you will learn that you can get away with vertical dissonance (a chord that is dissonant) if the horizontal lines (the melody, for instance) are smooth and make sense. You will also learn that an amazing amount of harmonic change and dissonance is acceptable when the chords are connected by a common tone, a note that occurs in adjacent chords.

If you don't like the sound of some of the dissonances at first, I suspect they will grow on you as you experi-

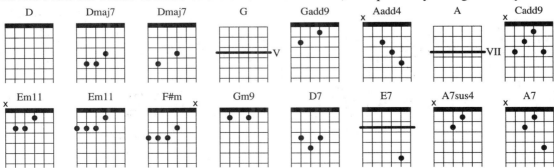

ment with them. Open tunings can help open up your ears to new harmonies. Give it a try!

Recordings in Open D (or Open E)

Artist	Tune	Source
Will Ackerman	Ely	Search for the Turtle's Navel
Allman Brothers	Little Martha	Eat A Peach
Eric Clapton	Give Me Strength	461 Ocean Boulevard
Bruce Cockburn	Sunwheel Dance	Sunwheel Dance
Ry Cooder	Vigilante Man	Into the Purple Valley
	Speedo	Border Line
John Fahey	Steel Guitar Rag	I Remember Blind Joe Death
Peter Frampton	Penny for Your Thoughts	Comes Alive
John Hammond	Dust My Broom	John Hammond Live
Richie Havens	Just Like A Woman	On Stage
	Handsome Johnny	Woodstock
John Lee Hooker	Terraplane Blues	Ultimate Collection 1948-1990
Robert Johnson	Preaching Blues	The Complete Recordings
Leo Kottke	Echoeing Gilewitz	A Shout Toward Noon
Adrian Legg	The Irish Girl	Guitars & Other Cathedrals
Dougie MacLean	Caledonia	Collection
Mary McCaslin	Circle of Friends	Circle of Friends
Dale Miller	Were You There	Both of Me
Joni Mitchell	Both Sides Now	Clouds
	Chelsea Morning	Clouds
Tracy Moore	Moonrise Lullaby	Skypiece
Nirvana	Lithium	Nevermind
Pearl Jam	Oceans	Ten
Chris Proctor	Wargames	Travelogue
Willis Alan Ramsey	Watermelon Man	Willis Alan Ramsey
Preston Reed	Overture (For Lily)	Metal
Roy Rogers	Bad Situation	Slide of Hand
	Stones in My Passway	Slide of Hand
Martin Simpson	Golden Vanity	Golden Vanity
Chris Smither	Mail Order Mystics	Happier Blue
George Thorogood	Woman With the Blues	Maverick
Chris Whitley	Look What Love Has Done	Living with the Law
David Wilcox	Mighty Ocean	Home Again

Related Tuning

D A d f# a c#´
Alex deGrassi	Midwestern Snow (E B e g# b d#´, -2)	Slow Circle

Open D Minor

D A d f a d´

Open D Minor tuning is simply a variation on Sebastopol tuning, Open D Major. The third string is lowered one half-step from Open D, making the tuning a minor sound instead of major.

We have already discussed that major and minor chord (often called "triads" because they consist of three notes) are made up of the first, third, and fifth notes of a *do-re-mi* scale. That means that the chord built on *do* consists of *do-mi-sol* (**do**-re-**mi**-fa-**sol**). The chord built on *re* consists of *re-fa-la* (the first, third, and fifth notes of a scale starting on *re*). The chord built on *mi* consists of *mi-sol-ti*, and so on. You get the idea.

The thirds of these chords are the notes that make the chords sound major or minor. D major consists of D-F#-A. D minor consists of D-F-A. *Do* and *sol* (the first and fifth notes) are the same in the two chords. But *mi* is the note that changes. D minor tuning is D A d f a d´; D major is D A d f# a d´. The only difference is the f-natural in D minor and the f# in D major.

Like Open D, D minor tuning is very rich and resonant, with the root note of the chord in the bass, as well as on the first string. The Eagles used D minor tuning on their recording "Bitter Creek." German fingerstylist Peter Finger used D minor tuning extensively early in his career.

Getting in Tune in D A d f a d´

If you are already in Open D tuning, simply lower the third string one half-step to f from f#. From standard tuning, lower the first, second, third, and sixth strings one whole-step.

One advantage of this tuning is that the three treble strings have the same relationships to each other as if they were in standard tuning! So any fingering you use on the three treble strings in standard tuning will work in D minor tuning as well. For instance, finger a normal end-of-the-neck D chord on the three treble strings. Now move it up the neck two frets, to the fourth and fifth frets. Strum all six strings. It should sound like a D major chord in Drop D tuning. (Remember, your sixth string is tuned down one whole-step also!)

The following charts provide the tuning information for D minor tuning.

Strings	Standard	DAdfad´	Change(s)	Fret to Match Adjacent Open String
1	e´	d´	Lower 1 whole-step	--
2	b	a	Lower 1 whole-step	5
3	g	f	Lower 1 whole-step	4
4	d	d	--	3
5	A	A	--	5
6	E	D	Lower 1 whole-step	7

35

Unison and Octave Tuning Chart--D A d f a d´

Now, go back through these two tuning charts for a moment and think about the three treble strings in standard tuning. These three notes: e´, g and b, make up an E minor chord. They also are the open treble strings in standard tuning. Even though you have lowered them all one whole-step for D minor tuning, you should still be able to visualize the three treble strings as if they were in standard tuning. Simply raise the fingerings two frets for D minor tuning.

Scales in D Minor Tuning

Again, be aware of your standard tuning fingerings on the three treble strings as you practice these scales. The notes are simply two frets lower than they would be in standard tuning. That may help you learn these fingerings quickly.

Since changing between major and minor mode within a song is quite common, I have also provided you with a D major scale in D Minor tuning.

D Minor Scale in Three Positions--D A d f a d´

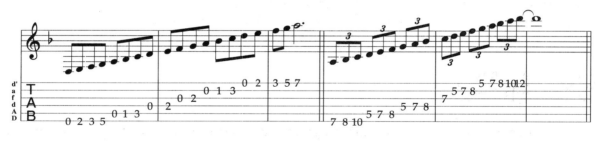

D Minor "Waterfall" Scale--D A d f a d'

D Major Scale--D A d f a d'

Chords in D A d f a d'

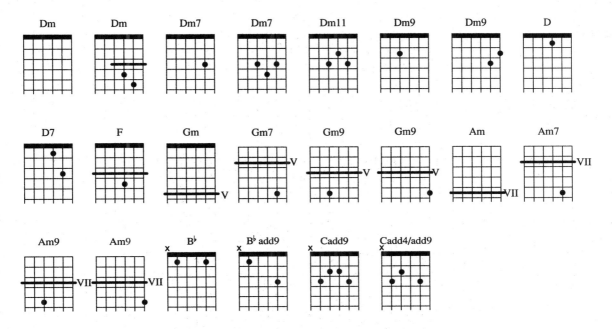

Nice Variations on Open D Minor

A beautiful variant of D minor tuning is Dm7. Singer and serious strummer Richie Havens uses this tuning on his tune "From the Prison." He drops his first string from d′ to c′, to produce D A d f a c′. Another nice voicing of Dm7 that will produce a slightly different sound is D A d f c′ d′, raising the second string three half-steps from a to c′.

Recordings in Open D Minor

Artist	Tune	Source
Eagles	Bitter Creek	Desperado
Peter Finger	For Ladies I Couldn't Get	Acoustic Rock Guitar
	Wishbone Ash	Acoustic Rock Guitar
Richie Havens	From the Prison	Richie Havens On Stage
Dm7 (D A d f a c′)		
Skip James	Hard Time Killing Floor	Early Blues 1931
Martin Simpson	Bonny At Morn	When I Was On Horseback
Bukka White	Aberdeen Mississippi Blues	Mississippi Blues

DAdead'

D A d e a d´ tuning is similar to D A D g a d´ in that one pair of strings is tuned only one whole-step apart, the distance of two frets. This proximity of notes allows for smooth scale playing (with some practice!) over those strings, either using consecutive open strings, or using a partial barre chord.

This tuning is used regularly by a number of Celtic style fingerpickers, as well as Kentucky fingerpicker and 1995 national fingerpicking champion Pat Kirtley.

Getting In Tune in D A d e a d'

From Open D tuning, simply lower the third string one whole-step from an f# to an e.

From standard tuning, lower the first, second, and sixth strings one whole-step, as you did for D A d g a d´, and Open D Major and D Minor. Lower the third string three half-steps from g to an e.

Once you have the guitar in tune, the second fret of the fourth string should equal the open third string.

The following charts show you how to tune to D A d e a d´ from standard.

Strings	Standard	DAdead´	Change(s)	Fret to Match Adjacent Open String
1	e´	d´	Lower 1 whole-step	--
2	b	a	Lower 1 whole-step	5
3	g	e	Lower 3 half-steps	5
4	d	d	--	2
5	A	A	--	5
6	E	D	Lower 1 whole-step	7

Unison and Octave Tuning Chart--D A d e a d´

Scales in D A d e a d'

The fingerings of the scales of D A d e a d´ are similar to D A d g a d´, in that there is a pair of strings that are only one whole-step apart.

This juxtaposition presents some interesting fingering possibilities when you play scales across the neck (bass to treble, for instance). For the time being, follow the tablature markings for suggested fingerings in each part of the neck.

Certainly, all of these scale fingerings can be moved to different strings, but I attempted to put them in the most playable settings. You may find fingerings that work better for you. Go for it!

D Major Scale in Three Positions--D A d e a d'

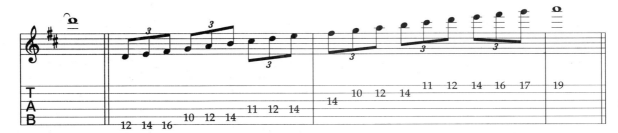

D Major "Waterfall" Scale--D A d e a d'

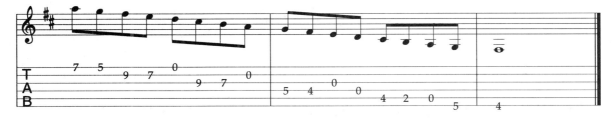

D Minor Scale in Three Positions--D A d e a d'

D Minor "Waterfall" Scale--D A d e a d'

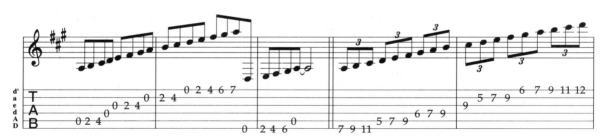

A Major Scales in Three Positions--D A d e a d´

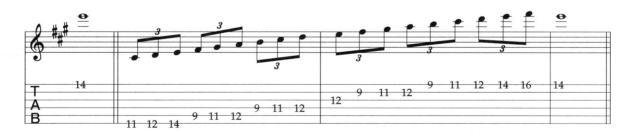

A Major "Waterfall" Scale--D A d e a d'

Chords in D A d e a d'

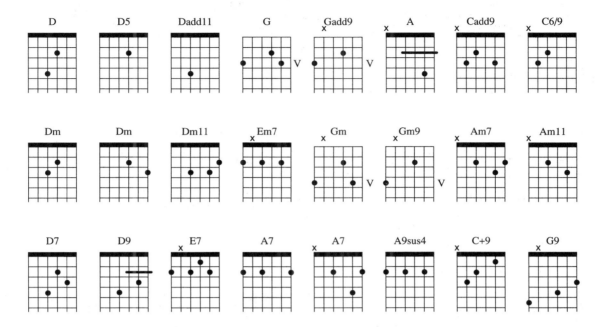

Recordings in D A d e a d'

Artist	Tune	Source
Michael Coulon	Path of Fallen Leaves	Crossing Paths
Alex deGrassi	Causeway (D A d e a d´, +2)	Slow Circle
Ed Gerhard	Blue Highway (B´ A d e a d´)	Luna
Pat Kirtley	Daisy Goes a Dancing	Kentucky Guitar
Joni Mitchell	I Had a King	Joni Mitchell
Bill Mize	Freefall	Tender Explorations

Related Tunings

Michael Hedges (D A d e a b)	Naked Stalk	Taproot
Michael Hedges (E A d e a d´)	Because It's There	Live on the Double Planet

D A d e a c#´
(Lower the first string one half-step)
D A d e a c´
(Lower the first string one whole-step)
B´ A d e a d´
(Lower the sixth string three half-steps)

Open G
DGdgbd'

Like Open D, Open G tuning has a long history.

This tuning is often called "Spanish" tuning. It is named after a 19th century piece in Open G tuning, entitled "Spanish Fandango." A brief history and the standard notation of the tune are included in the book *20th Century Masters of Finger-Style Guitar* (Hal Leonard Pubications). The tablature for Norman Blake's version of the tune is included in the same book.

Not only was Open G tuning popular among parlor guitarists of the 1800s, it also became a favorite of blues players in the early 1900s. It was favored by slide players, and continues to be to this day. A recent recording that includes Open G tuning with slide was the enormously popular *Eric Clapton Unplugged* recording.

Yet another tradition of guitar playing that uses Open G tuning is Hawaiian "Slack Key." Practitioners of this lovely style refer to Open G tuning as "Taro Patch."

Open G and Open D Tunings: Similar, But Different

Open G is similar to Open D tuning in that both are major chord tunings, with the same intervals between strings, in the same order. However, these intervals are shifted one string toward the treble as compared to Open D.

This shift accounts for a striking difference between the two: the root note of the open-string chord (the I chord, G) is not the lowest note in the bass. Rather, the fifth of a G chord--a D--is the lowest note of the tuning. Because of this, Open G tuning does not provide the rich, six-string, root-position tonic chord that Open D can produce. But, in its place, Open G can easily produce the common V-I bass progression (D-G) that is fundamental to much western harmony.

Like the bass string, the highest-pitched string of this tuning is tuned to the fifth (D) of the open-string chord, the G. Slide players, especially in the fingerpicking style, often play the melody on the first string, harmonizing it with open strings. If the lowest note of a melody is the fifth note of a scale (*sol*), and the upper note is somewhere near *sol* an octave higher, the melody will lie very nicely on the first string between the nut and the 12th fret.

Using the first string in Open G tuning, try playing the opening phrase of the melody to "Columbia, the Gem of the Ocean." Start the melody on the open string, immediately jumping to the fifth fret. Then the melody moves to the seventh fret and up to the twelfth, before descending again. You can see that this melody lies nicely on the first string in this tuning.

In Open D tuning, the first string is *do* in the key of D. For a melody that lies between *do* and the *do* an octave higher, Open D tuning is a nice one; the melody will lie entirely on the first string. Try playing the opening phrase of "Over the Rainbow" between the nut the twelfth fret in Open D tuning. Start with the open string and jump immediately to the twelfth fret. Harmonize it with the other open strings.The melody fits nicely on the first string in Open D tuning.

Now try the melody of "Over the Rainbow" in the same positions on the first string, but this time in Open G tuning. Use the open strings as harmony notes. It doesn't sound right, does it? That's because the comfortable range of a melody on the first string in Open G tuning is *sol* to *sol,* not *do* to *do* as it is in Open D tuning--and as it needs to be for "Over the Rainbow."

As you arrange songs in these tunings, figure out the range of the melody first. That may give you a hint as to which tuning might be easier to use for a particular song.

Rules are made to be broken, of course. There are plenty of arrangements on the guitar that have melodies that do not lie within the one octave range of the the first string. But, as you get started with arranging your own tunes, you might consider approaching the arrangements from this point of view.

Getting in Tune in Open G

You might have noticed that in standard tuning the open second, third, and fourth strings are the three notes of a G chord: d, g, and b. To arrive at Open G, you simply need to tune the other three strings to notes of a G chord as well.

From standard tuning, tune the first, fifth, and sixth strings down one whole-step. Now you are in Open G tuning. The following charts show you how to tune to Open G from standard, and how to fine-tune the tuning once you have arrived there.

Strings	Standard	DGdgbd´	Change(s)	Fret to Match Adjacent Open String
1	e´	d´	Lower 1 whole-step	--
2	b	b	--	3
3	g	g	--	4
4	d	d	--	5
5	A	G	Lower 1 whole-step	7
6	E	D	Lower 1 whole-step	5

Unison and Octave Tuning Chart--Open G (D G d g b d´)

43

Scales in D G d g b d'

To make the scales and chord fingerings of Open G digestable, think of the second, third, and fourth strings as standard tuning (which they are, of course!). Anything familiar like that that you can hold onto as you learn a new tuning is highly advisable.

From Double Drop D tuning (D A d g b d´), you already may be accustomed to the scales and chord fingerings on the four treble strings. They are the same in Open G tuning. The only difference between the two is the fifth string, which is lowered one whole-step when you switch from from D A d g b d´ to Open G.

Have fun experimenting with these scales.

G Major Scale in Three Positions--D G d g b d'

G Major "Waterfall" Scale--D G d g b d'

Chords in Open G

From Open D tuning, you will find that the scales and chords are the same in Open G, simply moved one string toward the treble. This is a wonderful realization for most practitioners of open tunings. Compare the chords of Open G and Open D. Can you see that they are similar?

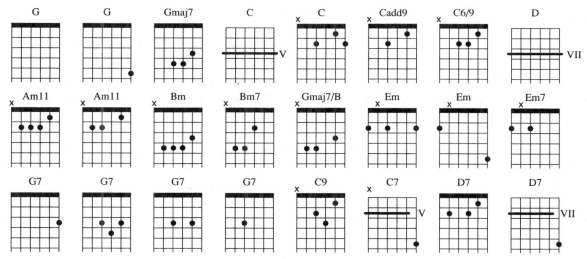

Recordings in Open G

Artist	Tune	Source
Dan Ar Bras	The Blood of the Boat	Acoustic
Barbeque Bob	Motherless Chile Blues (Open A)	Chocolate to the Bone
Rory Block	Crossroad Blues	High Heeled Blues
Peter Frampton	Show Me the Way	Comes Alive
Stefan Grossman	The Windblown Star	Love, Devils and the Blues
John Hammond	I Can't Be Satisfied	John Hammond Live
Wizz Jones	The First Girl I Loved	The Village Thing Tapes
Moses Kahumoku	Pohakuloa	Hawaiian Slack Key Masters
Ray Kane	Hawaiian Reverie	Master of the Slack Key Guitar
Jorma Kaukonen	Water Song	Burgers (Hot Tuna)
John Renbourn	The English Dance	Black Balloon
Martin Simpson	Charlie's Boogie	Nobody's Fault But Mine
James Taylor	Love Has Brought Me Around	Mudslide Slim
George Thorogood	Gear Jammer	Maverick
Chris Whitley	Phone Call From Leavenworth	Living with the Law

Related Tunings

There are many tunings that are related to Open G tuning. We will cover quite a number of them in the upcoming chapters. To simplify things, you can group the related tunings into two main categories: modes of G; and C-bass tunings.

For instance, in the upcoming chapters several tunings that we will cover simply change the second string of Open G tuning. That, of course, is the third of the chord, the note that makes the chord major or minor. So we will have G Minor tuning, G suspended fourth tuning, and G add9 tuning.

Other tunings use C on the sixth string. For instance, Open G tuning can have a wonderfully deep effect by simply tuning the bass string down to a C. You might still play in the key of G, but now the IV chord (C) has a low root note underneath it. A beautiful sound!

G sus4
D A d g c´ d´

This tuning is the same tuning as Open G, but with one difference: the second string is raised one half-step from standard, from b to c´.

This tuning is also called G suspended 4th, since the third of the chord (b) has been replace by the fourth note of the G scale (c´). This tuning contains the same intervals between strings as D A d g a d´ (or D suspended 4th).

The reason a guitarist might use D G d g c´ d´ instead of D A d g a d´ often lies with the pitch range of the melody. For singers this is an important consideration. The same melody in these two tunings will lie either an interval of a fourth (five half-steps) or a fifth (seven half-steps) away. This is a substantial range for most singers, and must be considered if tunings like this are being used to accompany vocalists.

D G d g c´ d´ and D A d g a d´ relate to each other much as Open G and Open D do. D G d g c´ d´ has the fifth on the bass string like Open G, and has the melody range of *sol* to *sol* on the first string. D A d g a d´ is like Open D in that the root is in the bass, and the melody range on the first string is *do* to *do*.

Because D G d g c´ d´ tuning does not explicitly state major or minor modalities (it does not have the third of a G chord as an open string), it is popular among players of Celtic music. In that style, the melodies often float better on top of an accompaniment that is neither explicitly major nor minor.

To Get in Tune in D G d g c´ d´

Like Open G tuning, tune the first, fifth, and sixth strings down one whole-step from standard tuning. Raise the second string one half-step to c´. If you often raise the pitch of the second string above standard tuning (b), consider using a lighter gauge string than normal to avoid breaking strings.

Strings	Standard	DGdgc´d´	Change(s)	Fret to Match Adjacent Open String
1	e´	d´	Lower 1 whole-step	--
2	b	c´	Raise 1 half-step	2
3	g	g	--	5
4	d	d	--	5
5	A	G	Lower 1 whole-step	7
6	E	D	Lower 1 whole-step	5

Unison and Octave Tuning Chart--D G d g c´ d´

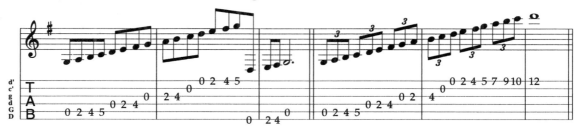

Scales in D G d g c' d'

Mostly guitarists play in the key of G in D G d g c´ d´ because the tuning is so similar to Open G. The key of G minor is relatively easy to use in this tuning as well.

The key of C is not difficult to use in this tuning, although you have no low-pitched, open-string root note in this tuning for the key of C. You can try tuning the bass string down a whole step to C to produce that low C, but that's another chapter!

G Major Scale in Three Positions--D G d g c d'

G Major "Waterfall" Scale--D G d g b d'

47

G Minor Scale in Three Positions--D G d g c d'

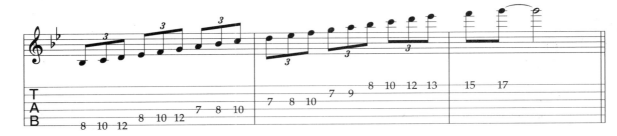

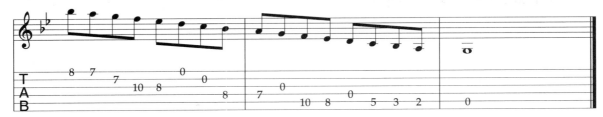

G Minor "Waterfall" Scale--D G d g c' d'

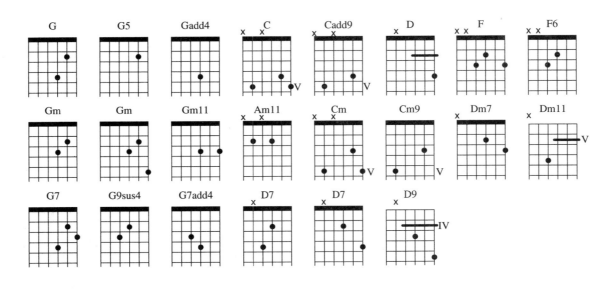

Chords in D G d g c' d'

The chords in this tuning are very similar to another suspended fourth tuning: D A d g a d´. Try moving the chord fingerings of D A d g a d´ one string toward the treble and see what happens.

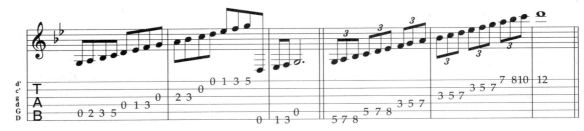

Recordings in D G d g c¹ d¹

Steve Baughmann	Planxty Bongwater	Owner's Daughter
Eric Schoenberg	Devrah's Delight	Steel Strings
	The Musical Priest	Acoustic Guitar
Martin Simpson	Betsy the Serving Maid	Band of Angels

Related Tunings

C G d g c´ d´
(Lower the bass string one whole-step to C)

D A d g c´ d´
(Raise the fifth string one whole-step to A)

Open G Minor
DGdgb♭d'

Open G minor is another favorite tuning of players of Celtic music. Great players like John Renbourn, Stefan Grossman, and Peter Finger have recorded extensively with this tuning.

The third of the chord--which is found on the second string in this tuning, and in Open G tuning--is lowered one half-step from Open G to produce the minor modality.

Open G minor has all of the advantages and disadvantages of Open G tuning. The lowest bass string is the fifth of the most common tonic chord (G minor), as is the open first string. The range of the melody on the first string is from *sol* to *sol,* rather than *do* to *do.* Because it is an open minor chord, other triadic minor chords can be played with one finger, simply as a barre fingering.

To play a major chord in this tuning, fret the second string one fret in front of a six-string barre. To play a G major chord in this tuning, simply fret the second string at the first fret.

Juxtaposing major and minor chords in a tuning like this can have a striking musical effect.

To Get in Tune In Open G Minor

If you are in Open G tuning, simply lower the second string one half-step from b to b-flat.

If you are in standard, lower the first, fifth, and sixth strings one whole-step from standard tuning, just as you did for Open G tuning. Lower the second string one half-step from standard tuning, from b to b-flat.

The following chart diagrams the strings that change from standard to produce Open G Minor, the amount that each string changes, and at which fret you depress each string to match its pitch with that of the adjacent open string.

Strings	Standard	DGdgb♭d'	Change(s)	Fret to Match Adjacent Open String
1	e'	d'	Lower 1 whole-step	--
2	b	b♭	Lower 1 half-step	4
3	g	g	--	3
4	d	d	--	5
5	A	G	Lower 1 whole-step	7
6	E	D	Lower 1 whole-step	5

The music example shows the pitch matching exercise in tablature, plus how to fine tune the instrument using octaves.

Unison and Octave Tuning Chart--D G d g b-flat d´

Scales in Open G Minor

This is our first attempt at playing scales with this pattern of intervals between the open strings. So there will be some slight shifting of frets, compared to what you are used to in standard tuning.

I have chosen to show the G Dorian scale in the following example. The reason for doing this is that most tunes that I have come across in this tuning are played in the Dorian mode. Dorian mode is a minor scale, but with the sixth note of the scale raised a half-step higher than it is in the natural minor scale. In the key of G minor, this gives you an E-natural instead of an E-flat. Because of the E-natural (the third of a C chord), Dorian mode provides a C major chord instead of a C minor in the key. If you read music, you might change the E-naturals to E-flats to practice playing in G "natural" minor.

G Minor (Dorian) Scale in Three Positions--D G d g b-flat d´

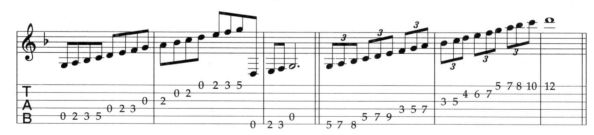

G Minor (Dorian) "Waterfall" Scale--D G d g b-flat d'

51

Open G Minor

Chords in Open G Minor

Celtic players using tunings like Open G Minor often will finger only melody notes, allowing open strings to ring in conjunction with the melody note. Look for Renbourn's "The Mist Covered Mountains of Home" (Stefan Grossman's Guitar Workshop) for a good example of this technique. Other common and useful chords are diagrammed in the following chart of chord fingerings.

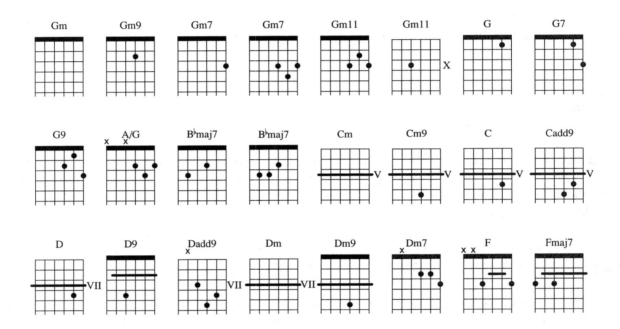

Recordings in Open G Minor Tuning

Artist	Tune	Source
John Fahey	Dance of Death	Dance of Death
	Summertime (+2)	I Remember Blind Joe Death
Peter Finger	Hope and Memory	Acoustic Rock Guitar
	Just a One-Man Band	Acoustic Rock Guitar
Stefan Grossman	Lament for a Goodman	Fingerpicking Delights
Laurence Juber	Diminished Returns	LJ
John Renbourn	Mist Covered Mountains of Home	Black Balloon
	Clarsach	The Hermit

Related Tunings

E A e a c´ e´ (Open A minor; which is Open G Minor +2)

D G d g b♭ c´

(Lower the first string one whole step from Open G Minor tuning.)

DGdgad'

Like D A d e a d´ and the suspended fourth tunings D A d g a d´ and D G d g c´ d´, this tuning has the distinctive feature of having the interval of a major second--one whole-step--between a pair of strings.

This tuning shares the same intervals with D A d e a d´, but moved one string toward the treble. So the fingerings for the scales and the chords will be similar, simply moved over one string.

What's In A Name?

You can call this tuning Gadd9, or G2 or Gsus2, or simply by its notes. Normally the name Gadd9 implies that you have an entire G triad (G, B, and D) to begin with, and you add the ninth (an A note) to it. However, in D G d g a d´ tuning, the third of a G chord--the B note--is not one of the open strings. Therefore, some people would suggest that the Gadd9 name is incorrect.

Some of these folks would suggest that the name be G2, which implies that the third is not present, but that the second degree of the scale--also A, just like the ninth--*is* present.

So why don't we call it G9, you ask? In modern terminology, a ninth chord implies that the chord is a dominant seventh to begin with (like C7 and G7), and the ninth note of the scale is added to it. The notes of a ninth chord are the first, third, fifth, seventh, and ninth notes of the scale. The sound of those five notes together is quite a bit more complex than we get from these notes: D, G, and A, which make up D G d g a d´ tuning.

In rock music, modern notation includes the name G5 for a G chord that has only roots and fifths, no thirds. (These most often are two- or three-note chords that are played on the bass strings, often with heavy distortion.) With that in mind, perhaps this tuning should be called G5add9.

Whatever you call it, I hope you have some fun with it. Again, you will find this tuning used by Celtic players, among others.

Getting in Tune in D G d g a d'

As you can see, this tuning is very close to Open G tuning. If you are in Open G, simply lower the second string one whole-step from b to a.

To produce D G d g a d´ from standard tuning, lower the first, second, fifth, and sixth strings one whole-step. As in all the previous chapters, I have provided the following charts to help you tune to this tuning, and to fine-tune your guitar once you have reached the pitches.

Strings	Standard	DGdgad´	Change(s)	Fret to Match Adjacent Open String
1	e´	d´	Lower 1 whole-step	--
2	b	a	Lower 1 whole-step	5
3	g	g	--	2
4	d	d	--	5
5	A	G	Lower 1 whole-step	7
6	E	D	Lower 1 whole-step	5

Unison and Octave Tuning Chart--D G d g a d´

Scales in D G d g a d´

There are a number of ways to look at this tuning to help you understand it. Each pair of strings--the first and second; the third and fourth; and the fifth and sixth--has the same relationship with each other as they do in standard tuning. All of these intervals are perfect fourths. So if you play two-note chords, or parallel scales going up or down the neck on one of these pairs of strings, it should "look" like standard tuning fingerings. However, as soon as you move from one set of these strings to another (from the second string to the third, or the fourth string to the fifth), the fingerings will have to shift two frets from where they occur in standard tuning.

Perhaps an easier way to view the this tuning is to think of the notes on the inner two strings (third and fourth) as standard tuning, and the notes on the other four strings fretted two frets higher than standard. You could also look at this tuning is as a close cousin of D A d g a d´. Except for the fifth string, all of the strings are the same notes in these two tunings. If you are familiar with D A d g a d´, D G d g a d´ won't be too difficult to learn. Practice these scales a bit, thinking of the fingerings on pairs of strings as the same fingerings as standard.

This tuning is another that can switch from major to minor with little difficulty. Hence two scales.

G Major Scale in Three Positions--D G d g a d´

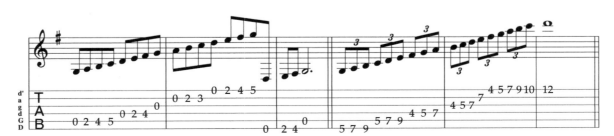

54

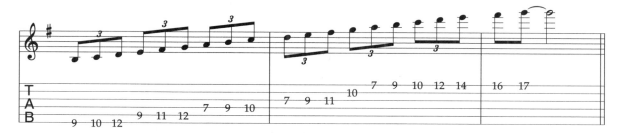

G Major "Waterfall" Scale--D G d g a d'

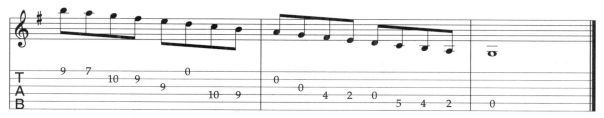

G Minor (Dorian) Scale in Three Positions--D G d g a d´

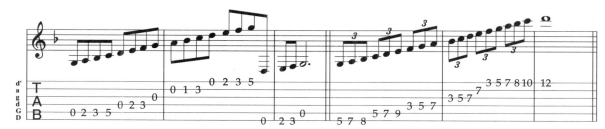

G Minor (Dorian) "Waterfall" Scale--D G d g a d'

Chords in D G d g a d′

As I stated earlier, the chords of this tuning are the same as D A d e a d′, but moved toward the treble string. Two-string chords (first/second strings; third/fourth; fifth/sixth) are like their standard-tuning cohorts.

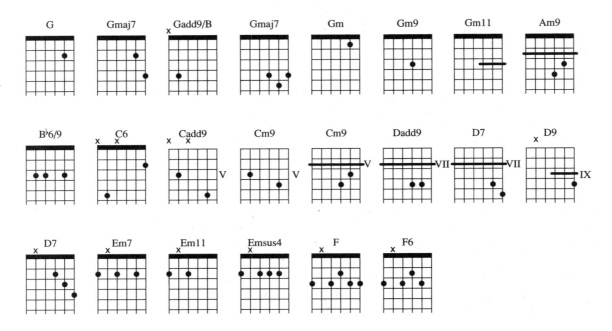

Recordings of D G d g a d′

Artist	Tune	Source
Dave Evans	Hewlett	Solos in Open Tunings
Dick Gaughan	MacCrimmon's Lament	No More Forever
Nanci Griffith	Ghost in the Music	Blue Moon
	One of These Days	True Believers

Related Tunings

D A d g a d′
(Raise fifth string one whole-step from D G d g a d′)
C G d g a d'
(Lower the sixth string one whole-step from D G d g a d′)

G6
DGdgbe'

This is a favorite tuning of guitar hall-of-famer Chet Atkins. It is very easy to use for players accustomed to standard tuning, because the four treble strings are still in standard tuning.

I think of this tuning as an Open G tuning, with the added sixth note of a G scale--e'--at the first string. Hence the name G6. It also is called "Drop G" tuning, going a step beyond Drop D, dropping the fifth string as well as the sixth one whole-step.

This tuning is great for the key of G, because you now have the root note of a G chord as an open string in the bass. When you play a G chord, you don't have to fret that bass note like you do in standard tuning. That leaves your fretting hand a bit freer to work with what is going on in the treble voices.

For example, in my book *The Art of Solo Fingerpicking*, I have arranged the fiddle tune "Devil's Dream" for fingerstyle guitar in G6 tuning. It works very well, since the fretting hand doesn't have to fret much in the bass. It can concentrate on the running eighth note melodies instead.

Fiddlers generally play "Devil's Dream" in A, so I simply place a capo at the second fret to play along with them.

Getting in Tune in DGdgbe'

It isn't difficult to tune to G6 tuning from standard. Simply tune both the fifth and sixth strings done one whole-step to G and D, respectively. The charts show the particulars.

Strings	Standard	DGdgbe'	Change(s)	Fret to Match Adjacent Open String
1	e´	e´	--	--
2	b	b	--	3
3	g	g	--	4
4	d	d	--	5
5	A	G	Lower 1 whole-step	7
6	E	D	Lower 1 whole-step	5

Unison and Octave Tuning Chart--D G d g b e´

Scales in D G d g b e'

Because the four treble strings are tuned the same as standard tuning, all the scales that you practiced in the Standard Tuning chapter early in the book work in G6, as long as you stay away from the two bass strings. Notes on the two bass strings must be fretted two frets higher than they are in standard.

Moving between two strings that are a fifth apart (like the fourth and fifth strings of this tuning) can present a fingering problem. There is good reason that "standard" tuning has developed largely using intervals of a fourth. Fourths allow the normal sized human hand to stretch far enough to reach all of the notes without leaving one position--without moving up or down the neck. When you have an interval of a fifth between two strings, you can wind up shifting positions horizontally as you move from one string to another. This type of movement takes some practice, of course, to make it smooth.

Spend most of your practice time with these scales working on the treble strings.

G Major Scale in Three Positions--D G d g b e´

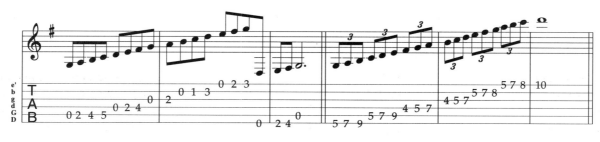

G Major "Waterfall" Scale--D G d g b e' (G6)

58

Chords in D G d g b e'

These fingerings will look quite familiar to those of you accustomed to standard tuning. As I have stated throughout this chapter, everything on the four treble strings is the same as standard.

Have fun experimenting with these, using the open bass strings to enrich the chords you play on the treble strings.

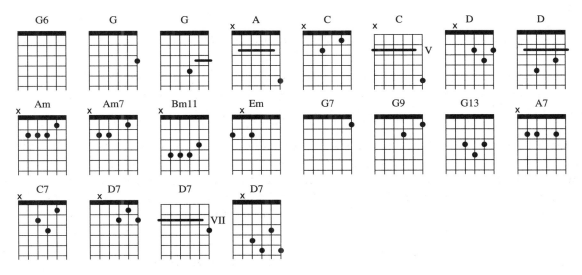

Recordings in G6 Tuning

Artist	Tune	Source
Muriel Anderson	Nola	Fingerstyle Guitar Magazine
Chet Atkins	Both Sides Now	Solid Gold '69; This Is Chet Atkins
	Yellow Bird	Class Guitar; This Is Chet Atkins
Duck Baker	The Dodder Bank	Opening the Eyes of Love
Doyle Dykes	Caleb's Report	Fingerstyle Guitar
Mark Hanson	Devil's Dream	Art of Solo Fingerpicking
Lonnie Johnson	Guitar Blues	Stepping on the Blues
Adrian Legg	A Candle in Notre Dame	Guitar for Mortals
Bill Mize	A Rose In A Fire	Tender Explorations
Tracy Moore	Tom Bombadil	Skypiece

Related Tunings

Ali Farka Toure (G6: G B d g b e´)	Cinquante Six	The Source
G Minor 6 (D G d g b-flat e´)		

CGdgbe'

C G d g b e' tuning is very closely related to the tuning in the previous chapter, G6. The five treble strings are the same in these two tunings, but the bass string is lowered one whole step below the D note of G6 tuning, to a low C. It is wonderful for playing in the key of C because of the low root note in the bass (C), and the fifth of a C chord (G) as the next lowest bass note. The four treble strings are still tuned like standard tuning.

This is a favorite tuning of Hawaiian players, among others. On the mainland, one of the better known examples of this tuning is Lindsay Buckingham's fingerpicking song "Never Going Back Again" from mid-'70s Fleetwood Mac. He capos way up the neck at the sixth fret to accommodate his singing and to give the guitar a very bright sound.

Getting in Tune in C G d g b e'

Starting with standard tuning, leave the four treble strings right where they are. Like G6 tuning, the four treble strings are the same pitches as standard tuning. Lower the fifth string one whole-step to G, and lower the sixth strings two whole-steps (four frets) to C.

The diagrams will show you how to get your guitar in tune in C G d g b e' tuning.

Strings	Standard	CGdgbe'	Change(s)	Fret to Match Adjacent Open String
1	e'	e'	--	--
2	b	b	--	5
3	g	g	--	4
4	d	d	--	5
5	A	G	Lower 1 whole-step	7
6	E	C	Lower 2 whole-steps	7

Unison and Octave Tuning Chart--C G d g b e'

One suggestion on a tuning like this: to make the fret numbers in the the chart work, you must already be close to the correct pitches of the tuning. If you tune the sixth string down first, the seventh-fret note on that string will not equal the open fifth string yet, as the chart says it should. You must tune the fifth string down first, matching the seventh fret of the fifth string to the fourth. Then tune the sixth string down and compare it to the already detuned fifth string. Then the chart numbers will make sense.

Another way to get to this tuning is to tune the sixth string down first, comparing it to the third fret of the fifth string, or the first fret of the second string. All of those notes are Cs. Then tune the fifth string down.

A basic rule: Begin retuning by tuning a string that is adjacent to a string that is *not* retuned. If all else fails, buy yourself an electronic chromatic tuner!

Scales in C G d g b e'

The scales of this tuning are identical to standard on the four treble strings. On the bass strings you will run into the same fingering problems that occurred in G6 tuning: Intervals of a fifth in the bass, which require bigger stretches in the fretting hand, or horizontal hand shifting. Luckily, most players don't play too many scale passages on the bass strings in this kind of tuning, using the notes as bass drones underneath the treble strings.

C Major Scale in Three Positions--C G d g b e′

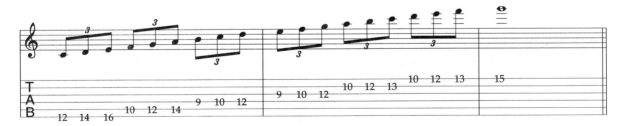

C Major "Waterfall" Scale--C G d g b e'

61

CGdgbe'

Chords in C G d g b e'

The chords are very rich in this tuning because of the low bass notes on the fifth and sixth string. Be aware that most often you will want to mute the open sixth string (C) when you are fingering a G chord with the open fifth string as the bass note. The low C will muddy the sound of a G chord.

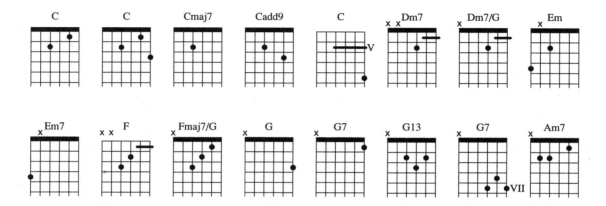

Recordings in C G d g b e'

Artist	Tune	Source
Chet Atkins	Flop-Eared Mule	Alone
Keola Beamer	Shells	Wooden Boat
Lindsay Buckingham	Never Going Back Again	Fleetwood Mac
Doyle Dykes	Mana Melody	Fingerstyle Guitar
Adrian Legg	The Cool Cajun	High Strung Tall Tales
Christopher Parkening	Sheep May Safely Graze	Parkening Plays Bach
Preston Reed	Flatonia	Instrument Landing, Metal
Richard Thompson	1952 Vincent Black Lightning	Rumor and Sigh

Related Tunings

Doug Smith   Shadowcasting   Labyrinth
(C A d g b e')
(From C G d g b e', raise the fifth string one whole-step.)

There are several other tunings closely related to C G d g b e'. We will cover a number of them in the upcoming chapters.

CGdgbd'

You can look at this tuning as a key-of-C tuning like the previous chapter, but with the first string tuned down to d'. In Hawaiian slack key, C G d g b d' is called C Wahine. Or you can look at it as an Open G tuning, with a low C in the bass. Joni Mitchell uses this tuning in her song "Cold Blue Steel and Sweet Fire."

C G d g b d' is great for playing in either the key of G or the key of C. Initially, you may be more comfortable using this tuning in the key of G, saving the low C for a rich bass note under the IV chord of the key.

Getting in Tune in C G d g b d'

From standard tuning, lower the first and fifth strings one whole-step. Lower the bass string two whole-steps (the equivalent of four frets).

Strings	Standard	CGdgbd'	Change(s)	Fret to Match Adjacent Open String
1	e'	d'	Lower 1 whole-step	--
2	b	b	--	3
3	g	g	--	4
4	d	d	--	5
5	A	G	Lower 1 whole-step	7
6	E	C	Lower 2 whole-steps	7

Unison and Octave Tuning--C G d g b d'

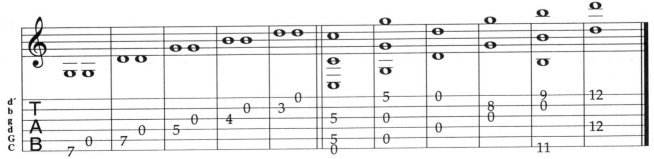

Scales In C G d g b d'

The scales in this tuning are identical to the scales in Open G tuning, except that the bass string notes are fretted two frets higher in this tuning.

Be aware that you will have the same fretting-hand stretch problems in this tuning as in the previous one: When the bass strings are tuned in fifths, the fretting hand has a lot of work to do to play scales on those strings!

G Major Scale in Three Positions--C G d g b d' (Open G, C bass)

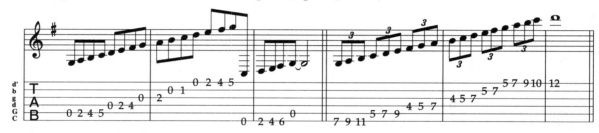

G Major "Waterfall" Scale--C G d g b d' (Open G, C bass)

C Major Scale in Three Positions--C G d g b d´

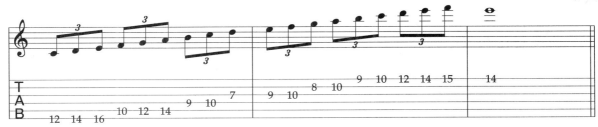

C Major "Waterfall" Scale--C G d g b d' (Open G, C bass)

Chords in C G d g b d'

The chords, like the scales, are identical to what you found in Open G tuning, except for the sixth string.

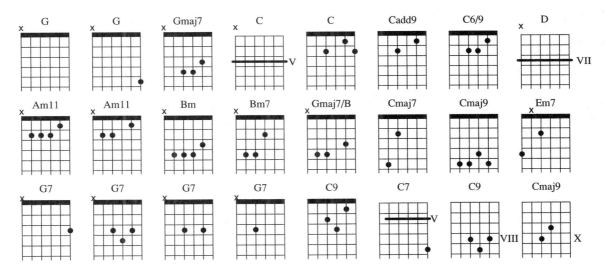

Recordings that Use C G d g b d'

Artist	Tune	Source
Sonny Chillingworth	Hi'ilawe	Sonny Solo
Leonard Kwan	Ke'ala's Mele	Hawaiian Slack Key Guitar Masters
Chris Proctor	Cheap Vacation	His Journey Home
Martin Simpson	Bob's Song	When I Was On Horseback

Related Tunings

C G d g b♭ d'
C G d g c' d'

Open C

CGcgc'e'

Open C is a favorite tuning of 12-string players, although it can be used to great effect on the 6-string as well. Leo Kottke, Peter Land, John Fahey, Tracy Moore, and other practitioners of the 12-string use or have used Open C. Kottke's tour de force "Busted Bicycle" from his 6- and 12-String Guitar album uses this tuning, lowered a minor third (three half-steps) below C! You need a great guitar and pretty meaty strings to make that sound good.

Another well know instrumental in Open C tuning (this time tuned down one whole-step below C) is folk singer Tom Rush's "Rockport Sunday." His vocal tune "No Regrets" uses the same tuning.

This tuning is different from the other major tunings we have covered so far--Open D and Open G--in that the third of the chord is on the first string. In Open D tuning, the third was on the third string. In Open G, the third was on the second string. The strings of these three tunings have the same intervals between them, in the same order, but all are offset by one string. In other words, the fingerings for the scales and chords will be the same one tuning to the next, but moved toward the treble one string as you move from Open D to Open G to Open C.

Getting in Tune in Open C

Raise the second string one half-step from standard. Lower the fourth and fifth strings one whole-step from standard. Lower the sixth string two whole-steps from standard.

Strings	Standard	CGcgc'e'	Change(s)	Fret to Match Adjacent Open String
1	e'	e'	--	--
2	b	c'	Raise 1 half-step	4
3	g	g	--	5
4	d	c	Lower 1 whole-step	7
5	A	G	Lower 1 whole-step	5
6	E	C	Lower 2 whole-steps	7

Unison and Octave Tuning--Open C (C G c g c e´)

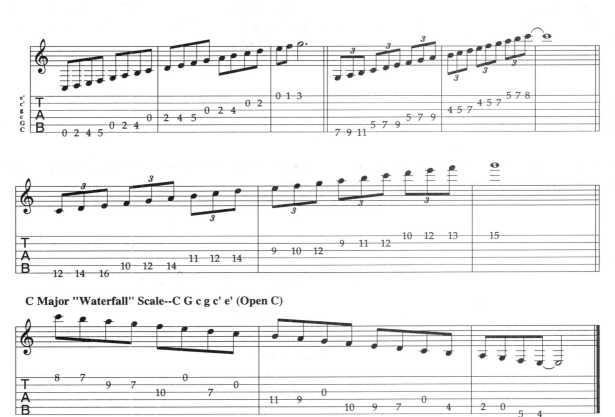

Scales in Open C

Again the scale fingerings here are similar to Open G tuning, simply moved one string toward the treble. Once again, be aware of the big stretches when you move from one bass string to the next.

C Major Scale in Three Positions--C G c g c´ e´

C Major "Waterfall" Scale--C G c g c' e' (Open C)

Chords

You can produce some great-sounding chords with simple fingerings in open tunings like this one. Experiment with some fingerings of your own. Or go back to the Open G and Open D chapters and try some of those fingerings moved toward the treble one or two strings, respectively.

Have fun!

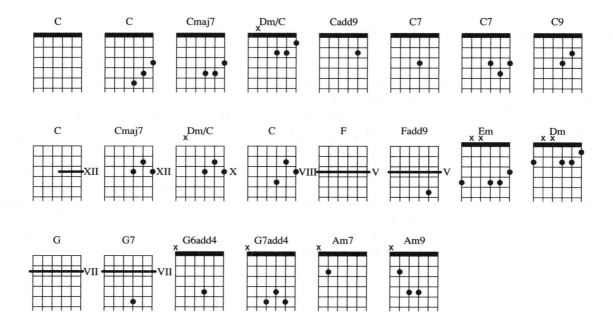

Recordings in Open C Tuning

Artist	Tune	Source
Bruce Cockburn	Foxglove	Night Vision
Peter Frampton	Wind of Change	Comes Alive; Shine On
Leo Kottke	Busted Bicycle	6- and 12-String Guitar
Peter Lang	St. Charles Shuffle	Fahey/Kottke/Lang
David Wilcox	Eye of the Hurricane	How Did you Find Me Here?

Related Tunings

Jimmy Page (C A c g c´ e´)	Bron-Y-Aur	Led Zeppelin III
Leonard Kwan (C G c g a e´)	Pau Pilikia	Leonard Kwan
Peter Lang (C G A g c´ e´)	V/The Connecticut Promissory Rag	Lycurgus

Open C Minor

CGcgc´e♭´

Another variant of Open C tuning, this tuning simply tunes the major third of a C chord, an e´ located on the first string, down to the minor third, an e-flat´.

Open C minor tuning is very similar to Open G minor and Open D minor, in that it has the same intervals between strings, simply moved toward the treble from the other two. Open D minor has its third on the third string; Open G minor tuning has its third on the second string; and Open C minor has the third on the first string. As you might anticipate (after having read through this many chapters of this book!), the scale and chord fingerings are the same from one of these tunings to another, simply moved one string toward the treble in this order: Open D minor, Open G minor, and Open C minor.

The advantage of Open C minor over the others is the richness afforded by the low C bass note. The open strings provide a root-position C minor chord (C in the bass). The open strings of Open D minor tuning also provide a root position chord, but the bass note is not quite as low as Open C minor. The open strings of Open G minor tuning have the fifth of the chord as the lowest bass note on the open sixth string.

Getting in Tune in Open C Minor

From Open C tuning, lower the first string one half-step from e´ to e-flat´. All of the others notes remain the same.

From standard tuning, lower the first string one half-step. Raise the second string one half-step. Lower the fourth and fifth strings one whole-step. And lower the sixth string two whole-steps.

Again, if you are concerned about raising a string--the second string in the case of Open C minor--consider putting on a lighter gauge string, or tune the entire guitar down one half-step to B´ F# b f# b d´.

Strings	Standard	CGcgc´e♭´	Change(s)	Fret to Match Adjacent Open String
1	e´	e♭´	Lower 1 half-step	--
2	b	c´	Raise 1 half-step	3
3	g	g	--	4
4	d	c	Lower 1 whole-step	7
5	A	G	Lower 1 whole-step	5
6	E	C	Lower 2 whole-steps	7

Unison and Octave Tuning--C G c g c´ e-flat´ (Open C Minor)

Scales in Open C Minor

As with several other tunings we have covered, there are some intervals of a fifth between strings in Open C minor tuning. Play through the accompanying scales, then move to the chords on page 71, where you really can take advantage of the richness a tuning like Open C Minor offers.

C Minor Scale in Three Positions--C G c g c' e-flat' (Open C Minor)

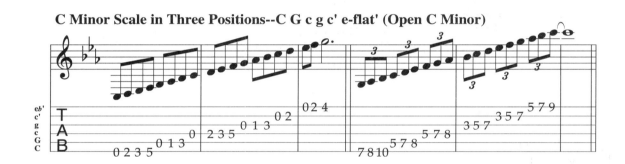

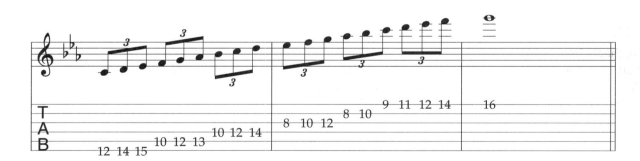

C Minor "Waterfall" Scale--C G c g c' e-flat' (Open C Minor)

Chords in Open C Minor

All the fingerings here are identical to Open C, except for the first string. To produce the same chord as you would get in Open C, fret the first-string notes one fret higher. To play a C major chord in this tuning, fret the first string at the first fret. To play any other major chord in this tuning, simply fret the first string at the first fret in front of a barre chord.

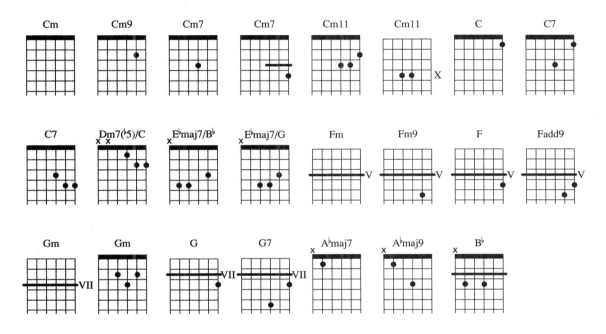

Recordings in Open C Minor

Artist	Tune	Source
Michael Coulon	Long Shadows	Crossing Paths
Laurence Juber	The Age of Rhythm	Between the Wars (Al Stewart)
Al Pettaway	Whispering Stones	Whispering Stones
Martin Simpson	Masters of War	Martin Simpson: The Collection

Other Tunings

There are about as many tunings in the world as there are guitar players. To cover them all in any depth would be impossible.

What I hope I have accomplished with the first section of the book was to provide enough information to help you gain a working knowledge of many of the most common and popular alternate tunings. In this chapter, I will list many more that may be of interest to you.

Remember to compare the tuning to standard to determine how to produce these. Most of the pitches are within three half-steps of standard pitch. Good luck experimenting with these. Don't break too many strings!

Tunings Close to Standard Tuning

This first group of tunings has only one string that has been altered from standard:

E A d f# b e′   Lower the third string one half-step from standard. It is often called "lute" tuning, since it was used in the lute era of the Renaissance. It was tuned three half-steps higher: G c f a d′ g′.

E A c# g b e′   Chet Atkins and John Knowles of Nashville refer to this tuning as "A9." It contains all five notes of an A9 chord. They used this tuning for their guitar piece "Honolulu Blue." Like other open-chord tunings, this one accommodates one-finger barre chords, as well as slide.

E G d g b e′   Lower the fifth string one whole-step. Arlo Guthrie used this tuning on his recording of "Motorcycle Song." Duck Baker used this tuning for "Fanteladdo."

E A d g a e′   A9sus4 tuning. Lower the second string one whole-step from standard. John Renbourn used it for "Country Blues" on his *Faro Annie* album. Ed Gerhard used it for his tune "Crow."

F A d g b e′   Raise the sixth string one half-step from standard. A great tuning for playing in the key of F: you don't have to fret the bass string on F chords. Michael Hedges ("Lenono") and Bert Jansch ("Lost Love") both have used this tuning.

E A e g b e′   Raise the fourth string one whole-step. Will Ackerman used this on "Tortion Bar." The three bass strings now act as they do in Open G tuning, with fifth string as the root note of the tonic chord. This is another A9 chord tuning, without the third, so it is as easy to play in the key of A minor as it is in A major.

E♭ A d g b e′   For tunes that move into not-so-friendly guitar keys like E♭ and Cm, this tuning works nicely. For chords with a fretted sixth string, the bass notes must be fretted one fret higher than normal. Try playing an E♭ chord with a first-position C fingering moved three frets higher than normal, to the fourth, fifth, and sixth frets. Finger the first string at the sixth fret with the little finger. Strum this, including the open sixth string E♭. Lovely.

D A d g b e′   Drop D. Hopefully you've read a full chapter on this tuning already!

C A d g b e′   A fabulous tuning for standard-tuning pieces in the key of C. All of the fingerings on the five treble strings are unaffected. You get a big fat C underneath your normal C fingering.

In the following tunings, two strings have been altered from standard.

D A D f# b e´   Lute tuning with a Drop D bass.

E A d g c´ f´   This is "all fourths" tuning. That means that there is an interval of a perfect fourth (five half-steps) between each pair of strings. A favorite tuning among some jazz players, because they don't have to compensate with the fretting hand for the major-third interval normally found between the second and third strings. Go back to the standard tuning scales on page 9 and notice how the tablature numbers shift as you move from the third string to the second. Now, tune the treble strings up one half-step each to c´ and f´. Lower the tablature numbers in the scales on page 9 by one fret on the second and first strings. Is this easier to play? Will Ackerman of Windham Hill used this tuning for "Bricklayer's Beautiful Daughter."

E A d e a e´   Asus4 tuning. "A Pipe" tuning, as it is called, was developed in Great Britain by Martin Carthy as a variation on D A d g a d´ tuning. Many of the traditional British melodies,which were accompanied so beautifully in D A d g a d´, were too high pitched for many singers in that tuning. So Carthy and others kept the intervallic relationships of D A d g a d´, but moved them one string toward the bass. This maintained the advantages of the suspended fourth tuning, but pitched the songs five half-steps lower than D A d g a d´.

Other Open Chord Tunings

You can invent tunings of you own that will sound good as open-string chords. All you need to know is the names of the notes of your chords. I've provided you with a chart for that purpose. With the accompanying chart, you should be able to devise a few of your own. The chart shows the first, third, fifth, seventh (dominant and major7th), and ninth for each chord. Mix and match the notes as you see fit. The advantage of these tunings is that you can finger other chords with a simple barre fingering.

E G# d e b e´   Open E7 tuning.

E B d g b e´   Open Em7 tuning.

D G d f# b d´   Gmaj7 tuning from the slack key tradition.

E A e a c´ e´   A minor tuning.

E A e g c´ e´   Am7 tuning.

E A e g# b e´   Amaj9 tuning, without the third.

E A c# g# b e´   Amaj9 tuning *with* the third.

E C e g c´ d´   Cmaj9 tuning used by Alex deGrassi.

Eᵇ C eᵇ g c d´   Cm9 tuning, same as Cmaj9,but minor.

D A d f# a c#   Dmaj7 tuning used by deGrassi.

D A d f# a e´   Dmaj9 tuning.

Chord Notes				
Chord __1__	__3__	__5__	__7__	__9__
A: A	C#	E	G/G#	B
Am: A	C	E	G	B
C C	E	G	Bᵇ/B	D
Cm: C	Eᵇ	G	Bᵇ	D
D: D	F#	A	C/C#	E
Dm: D	F	A	C	E
E E	G#	B	D/D#	F#
Em: E	G	B	D	F#
F: F	A	C	Eᵇ/E	G
Fm: F	Aᵇ	C	Eᵇ	G
G: G	B	D	F/F#	A
Gm: G	Bᵇ	D	F	A

Spend time experimenting with these tunings. Also, spend some time with the tunings listed for Will Ackerman, Michael Hedges, and John Renbourn. Chord fingerings for a number of their tunings are shown in the Chord Supplement section near the back of the book. For unison tunings--where at least one pair of strings is tuned to the same pitch--see the listings for Sonic Youth and Michael Hedges in the back of the book. Hedges' tunings also provide insight into dissonance--where two strings are tuned merely one half-step apart.

Playing Slide Guitar in Open Tunings

Slide and blues guitarists have used open-chord tunings for a long time. The ease of using an open-chord tuning, plus the fact that a full chord can be played with a bottleneck lying straight across the strings, make these tunings very attractive.

The most common tunings for slide guitar are Open G (D G d g b d´) and Open D (D A d f# a d´). Common variants of these two are Open A and Open E, respectively.

The latter two tunings are pitched one whole-step above their relatives. Certainly, the higher pitches provide a brighter, more strident tone, but they place considerably more stress on the instrument. Be careful if you tune up to Open A or Open E. Try lighter gauge strings if you are concerned about the structural integrity of your guitar. Or, to avoid this stress, consider placing a capo at the second fret on the lower-pitched tunings to create Open A and Open E.

Minor tunings also work well with a slide. D minor and E minor tunings (with the root notes on the first and sixth strings) were used by Elmore James and Bukka White, among others.

Some "Tricks" of Playing Blues Slide in Open D and Open G

As you study blues slide guitar in Open D and Open G, you will find that the most commonly played chords are full barre chords at the fifth, seventh, and twelfth fret, along with the open strings. These positions correspond to the I, IV, and V chords of the key.

Often, the notes at the third and tenth frets are incorporated into a slide tune as well. These notes help a tune to sound a little bluesier, since these notes correspond to "blue" notes of a major scale: the lowered third and the lowered seventh.

Another important stylistic consideration when playing the blues in an open tuning is to "scoop" up to the regular pitches. Try placing your slide one fret below each of the positions mentioned in the previous paragraphs, then slide up one fret to the normal position. For instance: slide from the fourth fret up to the fifth; from the sixth fret to seventh; and the eleventh to the twelfth. It doesn't take a lot of effort to make open D and Open G tunings sound bluesy with a slide.

With all of these things in mind--and after a little experimentation on your part--go back to some of your favorite slide recordings and listen for the fret positions played with the slide. You may be able to pick then out quickly, now that you understand the tendencies of blues slide players

Fingerpicking Slide

Many fingerpicked slide tunes, like Leo Kottke's "Watermelon" (*6- and 12-String Guitar*), don't necessarily adhere to the III, V, VII, X, and XII positions that blues players favor. These tunes will often have a single-line melody on the first string, played by the slide, with the accompaniment consisting largely of open strings.

Even in these non-blues tunes, the full-barre sound of a slide and some bluesy "scooping" from one fret below most often are incorporated, simply because it sounds so good.

Other Useful Slide Tunings

Speaking of Kottke again, he most often plays his slide tunes in Open G or Open D tuning (oftentimes tuned somewhat lower than standard pitch). But he plays his well-known version of "Louise" in Drop D tuning.

He succeeds at this in two ways: he largely avoids full barres with the slide; and, he plays melody notes with the slide on the treble strings while picking the open fifth and sixth strings as drones. When Kottke does barre all the way across the strings, he picks mostly the three bass strings, giving the illusion that he is in an Open D tuning.

Other guitarists play slide in standard tuning. Most often these are "lead" guitar players who have some sort of harmonic accompaniment behind them. They play one, two , or three notes at a time for the simple reason that more chord tones than that don't line up on one fret.

Slide guitar is played in other tunings and in other styles, but it is most often associated with the blues. A slide on guitar strings has the ability to imitate the scoops and moans of blues singers, something that ordinary fretting of the notes cannot duplicate.

> *The most common tunings for slide guitar are Open G and Open D.*

Other Blues Tunings for Slide Guitar

Since the basic harmony of the blues is most often a dominant seventh chord (G7 and A7, for example), let's try tuning one of the open strings to a note that produces a dominant seventh.

The notes of a G chord are G, B, and D, the first, third, and fifth notes of a G scale. The seventh note of a G scale normally is F#. To make the chord bluesy sounding, however, the seventh note must be one whole-step below a root note, so the seventh in a G7 chord is an F-natural. (An F# added to a G chord makes it a Gmaj7 chord--a decidedly un-bluesy sound!)

Let's experiment a bit with Open G, to determine which string you might want to change to an F for G7 tuning.

The notes of Open G are D G d g b d´. There are two root notes (G; *do*), one third (b; *mi*), and three fifths (D; *sol*). One of these notes we will change to an F. First, look at what notes of the chord are doubled or tripled. There are two G's, so one could be altered. There is only one b--the third of the chord--which makes the chord major or minor. If you change that note, the open strings will no longer sound like a G major chord. So let's leave that one alone. We also have three D's. We certainly can afford to change one of those to an F. Let's see if it works.

First, try changing the bass string up to an F. There are two disadvantages of this: You now have the seventh in the bass--a third inversion chord--and an uncommon voicing in the blues. In classical music, a third inversion normally has a very well-defined resolution, one that is seldom heard in the blues. Also, you are pulling the bass string above its normal standard-tuning pitch. Some extra stress will be apparent. So let's leave the bass string at D.

Second, try raising the fourth-string d note to an f. You will need an extra light string to stretch it up that far. I don't recommend it. Better, let's try lowering the third-string g to an f. This voicing is interesting. Perhaps worth investigating.

We have already decided that the second string should stay where it is. So, let's try raising the first string to an f´. As with putting an f on the fourth string, raising the first string to f´ puts extra stress on the string. You will have to determine whether or not you want to do this.

So the two possibilities that I see for a G7 tuning are these: D G d f b d´; and D G d g b f´. Experiment with them. I suspect that you may develop an affinity for them.

Slide Guitar

D7 Tuning

To make a D7 tuning out of Open D, let's go through the same process. In Open D tuning there are three open-string D's (first, fourth, and sixth strings); two A's (second and fifth strings) and one F# (third sting). The F# is the third of the chord, so let's leave that one alone. The note we need to make D into a D7 is a C.

Lowering the sixth string from D to C gives you the same third-inversion problem that you had in Open G. Raising the fifth from A to C is also impractical because of the string tension. Lowering the fourth string from D to C is a possibility. The other two possibilities are raising the second string to c′, or lowering the first string to c′.

Here are the three Open D7 tuning possibilities that I see: D A c f# a d′; D A d f# c′ d′; D A d f# a c′. Experiment with them all to see which voicing you like the best. As a point of interest, folk singer Richie Havens has recorded "The Dolphins" using D A d f# a c′.

Most slide players use the tried and true Open G and Open D tunings for slide. But if you want to develop a "Voice" of your own, you might consider experimenting with an Open 7th tuning. Have fun!

Slide Players to Hear

Two huge stars on the pop music scene, Eric Clapton and Bonnie Raitt, are sterling slide guitarists. Former Beatle George Harrison is another fine slide player whose playing regular turns up on the hit parade. Recordings of the great Delta slide players like Robert Johnson are also readily available to most album buyers.

Stefan Grossman's Guitar Workshop in Sparta, New Jersey, has a wealth of information on blues guitar players. Not only does he provide access to videos of great players past and present, but he has many teaching courses designed to help you learn to play like some of the greats. Some of the players he covers include: Muddy Waters, Blind Willie Johnson, Robert Johnson, Jesse Fuller, Tampa Red, Fred McDowell, Son House, Bukka White, Mance Lipscomb, Johnny Shines, Furry Lewis, and Blind Willie McTell.

If you are just beginning to play slide in open tunings, a great record to listen to is John Fahey's *I Remember Blind Joe Death*. This recording contains easily accessible slide pieces, mostly in Open E tuning. Another great recording for slide playing in open tunings is *John Hammond Live*.

Slide Recordings

Eric Clapton	While My Guitar Gently Weeps	Beatles White Album
	Walking Blues	Unplugged
Ry Cooder	Vigilante Man	Into the Purple Valley
	Thirteen Question Method	Get Rhythm
John Fahey	The Evening Mysteries of Ferry Street	I Remember Blind Joe Death
Leo Kottke	Louise	Greenhouse
Bonnie Raitt	Thing Called Love	Nick of Time
Roy Rogers	Tip-Walk	Slidewinder
Martin Simpson	Granuaille	When I Was On Horseback
	Charlie's Boogie	Nobody's Fault But Mine

Hawaiian "Slack Key"

The Slack Key Style

Hawaiian "Slack Key" guitar is currently enjoying a wave of popularity previously unbeknownst to the style. In a relatively short time, this acoustic folk fingerpicking style has made its way from the secluded family music rooms of native Hawaiians to major stages around the world.

This beautiful style of guitar playing is a microcosm of the Islands themselves. Mush of the playing is relaxed, but it can as uptempo and spirited as most any other fingerpicking style.

The term "slack key" actually refers to the detuned strings. The original native Hawaiian players of the guitar-- who had learned of the guitar through the Spaniards who helped build a cattle industry in Hawaii--tuned the strings lower than standard to better depict the native music on the instrument.

The players of the style became quite secretive of the tunings. This was especially true when natives realized that very little of their heritage would remain after the onslaught of westerners. Slack key guitar was a strictly Hawaiian style, one to be protected.

This attitude gradually changed, until players of the style began writing teaching books on slack key, and recording teaching videos. These days, with the support of Dancing Cat Records, the Hawaiian slack key style is influencing guitarists around the world.

The Tunings

Pianist and Dancing Cat founder George Winston has conducted extensive research into slack key style of playing and its tunings. The most common tunings are "Taro Patch" (Open G), "C Wahine" (C G d g b d´), and G Wahine (D G d f# b d´). These tunings account for over three-quarters of the slack key music that has been recorded. Another popular tuning is C Mauna Loa (C G e g a e´).

I will provide you with tuning charts for several of these tunings.

Taro Patch Tuning (Open G)

Strings	Standard	DGdgbd´	Change(s)	Fret to Match Adjacent Open String
1	e´	d´	Lower 1 step	--
2	b	b	--	3
3	g	g	--	4
4	d	d	--	5
5	A	G	Lower 1 step	7
6	E	D	Lower 1 step	5

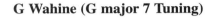

You will discover that these tunings are most often in major keys. Often the tuning includes a major sixth or seventh note, added to the major triad. In fact "Wahine" means that a major seventh has been added to a tuning. So the tuning of C Wahine is largely a C chord, but with a B in it (the major seventh), as well as the ninth (D). G Wahine is Open G tuning with the third string tuned down one half-step to F#, its major seventh.

"Mauna Loa" tuning is a major tuning that has the interval of a fifth (seven frets) between the two treble strings.

G Wahine (G major 7 Tuning)

Strings	Standard	DGdf#bd´	Change(s)	Fret to Match Adjacent Open String
1	e´	d´	Lower 1 whole-step	--
2	b	b	--	3
3	g	f#	Lower 1 half-step	5
4	d	d	--	4
5	A	G	Lower 1 whole-step	7
6	E	D	Lower 1 whole-step	5

Sonny Chillingworth

D Wahine (D A d f# a c#´)

Strings	Standard	CGdgbd´	Change(s)	Fret to Match Adjacent Open String
1	e´	d´	Lower 1 whole-step	--
2	b	b	--	3
3	g	g	--	4
4	d	d	--	5
5	A	G	Lower 1 whole-step	7
6	E	C	Lower 2 whole-steps	7

C Wahine (C G d g b d´)

Strings	Standard	CGdgbd´	Change(s)	Fret to Match Adjacent Open String
1	e´	d´	Lower 1 whole-step	--
2	b	b	--	3
3	g	g	--	4
4	d	d	--	5
5	A	G	Lower 1 whole-step	7
6	E	C	Lower 2 whole-steps	7

C Mauna Loa (C G e g a e´)

Strings	Standard	CGegae´	Change(s)	Fret to Match Adjacent Open String
1	e´	e´	--	--
2	b	a	Lower 1 whole-step	7
3	g	g	--	2
4	d	e	Raise 1 whole-step	3
5	A	G	Lower 1 whole-step	9
6	E	C	Lower 2 whole-steps	7

G Mauna Loa D G d d g d´

Strings	Standard	DGddgd´	Change(s)	Fret to Match Adjacent Open String
1	e´	d´	Lower 1 whole-step	--
2	b	g	Lower 2 whole-steps	7
3	g	d	Lower 5 half-steps	5
4	d	d	--	0
5	A	G	Lower 1 whole-step	7
6	E	D	Lower 1 whole-step	5

Ray Kane

How to Design Your Own Alternate Tuning

There is a wealth of alternate tunings that have already been invented and explored. You have explored many of them already in this book! Certainly you could spend all of your experimentation time with tunings developed by other artists. But there may be a time when the tunings you know simply aren't sufficient for a tune that you want to play. That's when you may want to make up a tuning of your own. This is how I suggest you start.

Does the Music Dictate the Tuning or Vice Versa?

A friend of mine watched Michael Hedges come up with a tuning in a guitar store using a new guitar he was buying. Being the creative musician that he is, Hedges reacted to the feel and sound of the small-bodied guitar with several new musical ideas. He began experimenting with the guitar tuning so that he could more easily play the music that was taking shape in his head.

He experimented rapidly, tuning one string up and another down. When he finally reached a tuning that had workable fingerings for the tune he had in his head, he found he was in a very common tuning: D A d g a d´.

This story is a good example of the music dictating what tuning the instrument needs to use. Rather than starting with a tuning, and perhaps being limited in musical choices by the tuning, Hedges started with the music, and made the guitar tuning work to project the tune.

Other players will approach composition from the opposite direction. They will change the tuning on their guitar with the expressed purpose of letting the tuning suggest a new piece of music. Once they have found a new tuning that sounds interesting, they will improvise until the chord formations and the sequence of notes they happen to play suggest melodies.

Your Goal

These two approaches are in sharp contrast. I would suggest that ultimately your goal is to have the music dictate the tuning. Let the musical ideas rattle around in your head for a bit, then sit down with the instrument and experiment. Think of Beethoven and his famous walks in the Vienna Woods, listening to the birds, searching for melodic ideas. Then he would go home and bang for hours on the piano, improvising on his original ideas until his piece took shape.

English fingerstyle virtuoso John Renbourn told me an interesting story about how one of his tunings developed. The first section of his tune "Palermo Snow" started out in Drop-D tuning, in the key of D minor. A new section of music was set in the key of G minor, which uses a B-flat rather than a B-natural note in its scale. The open B-string on the guitar was a problem in the key of G minor, so he tuned his second string down from B to B-flat to facilitate playing in the new key. It worked very well.

Because of the change of pitch on the second string, Renbourn's chord fingerings changed in the original D minor section, but only slightly (by one fret on the second string). This was much less of a problem than playing the G minor section with an open B-natural string. So his final tuning for "Palermo Snow" became D A d g b♭ e´.

Your First Experiments

To get started experimenting with your own new tunings, change just one or two strings from standard. That way you will still be close to standard tuning, where you know your way around, and you won't have to strain to figure out new chord formations and scales.

For instance, let's start by lowering the first string from E to D. If you strum a first-position E fingering in this tuning, you get an E7 sound without adding your little finger on the second string, third fret. Since the blues style is full of 7th chords, let's try a blues tune in this tuning: E A d g b d´.

The following is a 12-bar blues chord progression in the key of E major. Each chord gets four beats.

Key of E Blues

E7 / A7 / E7 / E7 /

A7 / A7 / E7 / E7 /

B7 / A7 / E7 / E7

For an E7 chord, simply play an E major fingering in the first position. The d´ on the first string provides the seventh of the chord.

For an A7 chord, play a first position A7 fingering: fretting the second fret of the second and fourth strings. This is a great chord in this tuning. The third of the A7--c#´--is juxtaposed against the d´ on the first string, a half-step above it. You may or may not like this dissonance, but give it a chance. If you don't like it, fret the second fret of the first string along with the other two notes. Or you can barre four strings at the second fret, and fret the first string at the fifth fret with your little finger.

For a B7 chord, finger a normal first-position B7, but don't fret the first string. Leave that open. You produce a B7 (#9), a chord that rock and rollers use regularly. If you don't like that sound, mute the first string, or don't pick it is you play the B7. Have fun!

More Experiments

E A d g b d´ tuning could also work well for a tune in the key of E minor. With a simple E minor fingering, you now have an Em7 chord. The tuning gives you a gorgeous Am11 chord with a simple Am7 fingering, and it provides easy access to two B chords: an easy Bm7, and that rock and roll B7(#9).Experiment with your standard-tuning chord fingerings, listening to what the retune first string does to each chord. You may like a first-position C chord with the D on top. Try lifting your index finger off the second string as you play C. The two treble strings, b and d´, combine with the rest of the C chord to give you a beautiful Cmaj9. Try this chord progression, for example: Em7-Am11-Cmaj9-B7(#9)-Em7.

Once you have explored this tuning, try retuning a different string. For instance, tune the second string down from b to a. Now your tuning is E A d g a d´. I can see nice possibilities for chords in the keys of E minor and A minor with this tuning. If you tuned your bass string up to B, you would have a favorite David Crosby tuning: E B d g a d´. He used this for his well-known tunes "Guinnevere" and "Deja Vu."

The Importance of Setting Parameters

Famed classical composer Igor Stravinsky always set parameters for each piece that he wrote: the style, the tonality, and such. Do the same thing when you experiment with new tunings. Ask questions like: What style do I want to use: rock and roll, Celtic, blues? What mood am I depicting: happy, sad, angst-ridden? These kinds of questions can suggest the kind of tuning that will best produce the effect that you want.

Perhaps the easiest way for me to explain this process is to describe my thinking as I composed a fingerstyle guitar solo piece of my entitled "Strawberry Curl." The first section of the tune is printed here.

"Strawberry Curl"

I needed an uptempo fiddle-tune piece for my second book, *The Art of Solo Fingerpicking*. This book consists of alternating-bass solo guitar pieces, so I had those parameters to begin with: alternating bass, uptempo, a running-eighth-note melody like a fiddle tune, and playability.

I decided immediately that I should drop the bass string down to D, so that I could alternate the bass in octaves (sixth and fourth strings) without having to fret anything with my left hand. That way my left hand would be free to fret the quick melody notes. Another parameter set: the piece would be in the key of D.

As I drove on the freeway one day, the first part of the melody came into my head. I hummed and whistled it over and over, picturing in my mind where the notes would lie on the fretboard. When I got home, I played the melody in different positions on the neck, looking for smoothness and playability. The fingerings worked better around the seventh fret than at the end of the neck, except for the few notes surrounding the high B in measure 2.

After more experimentation, I decided there wasn't one fingering in Drop D tuning that was easy enough to play at a high speed. So I began thinking about retuning.

The only real fingering problem I had was on the first string, so I tried tuning the first string down to d´. That moved the notes on the first string up two frets. *Voila!* This change placed the first-string notes on frets that were easy to reach as the melody moved between the second and first strings. As an added bonus, I had another open D string in a key-of-D piece--not a bad situation to have.

I came up with the second and third sections of the piece after I had arrived at the tuning. I liked the fingering so much for the opening melody that I didn't want to compose a new section that required changing the tuning. So I made sure I kept the new sections in keys that are closely related to D. Section 2 is in the key of B minor, the relative minor, and the third section is in D minor.

If you are interested in the entire version of this tune and a recording of it, *The Art of Solo Fingerpicking* is available at your local retailer (distributed by Music Sales). It also can be ordered directly from Accent On Music.

"Strawberry Curl"

Mark Hanson

Artists' Tunes and Tunings

We have compiled an immense numbers of tunes and tunings for this book.

The artists covered are diverse. There are '60s rockers, represented by the Beatles, Rolling Stones and Buffalo Springfield; and there are classical guitarists, represented by Christopher Parkening.

There are also fantastic fingerstyle soloists, like John Renbourn, Laurence Juber, and Leo Kottke; blues legends like John Lee Hooker; younger generation blues powerhouses like John Hammond and Rory Block; folk singers like Richie Havens, and slack key artists like Keola Beamer.

Also, we have an extensive list of tunings from such contemporary rock groups as Sonic Youth, Sound Garden, and Pearl Jam. There is a little something here for everyone.

We did not have room to present an extensive list from each of the 180 artists listed in the following pages. What we tried to do was offer as wide a range of tunings from each artist as possible.

Have a great time working through these tunings. Again, you may find one that does everything that you need. Stick with it. Learn all of the ins and outs of that tuning, so that you can play in that tuning as well as others play in standard.

Or, immerse yourself in the sheer volume of possibilities here. It's fun to dive into a new tuning and have no idea where you are. It's challenging and exciting to see if you can make music out of a totally new tuning.

Have fun!

Clockwise from upper left:
Doyle Dykes, John Renbourn,
Laurence Juber, Keola Beamer,
and Alex deGrassi.

Artists' Tunes and Tunings

TITLE	TUNING	ALBUM
ACKERMAN, WILLIAM		
Barbara's Song	C$^{\#}$ G$^{\#}$ c$^{\#}$ g$^{\#}$ c$^{\#}$´ e´	Search For The Turtle's Navel
Bricklayer's Beautiful Daughter	E A d g c´ f´	It Takes A Year
Ely	Open D	Search For The Turtle's Navel
Gazos	C A d f$^{\#}$ a c$^{\#}$´	Search For The Turtle's Navel
Impending Death Of The Virgin Spirit	C$^{\#}$ A c$^{\#}$ g$^{\#}$ a e´ Capo II	Search For The Turtle's Navel
Innocent Moon	E E A e b e´	Imaginary Roads
It Takes A Year	D G d g a d´	It Takes A Year
Singing Crocodile	G$^{\#}$´ G$^{\#}$ e f b d$^{\#}$	Conferring With The Moon
Windham Mary	F A^{b} c e^{b} a^{b} e^{b}´	Search For The Turtle's Navel
Wondering Again	D A D g a d´	Imaginary Roads
ALEXANDER, CHARLES DAVID		
Orange Blossom Special	G6 (D G d g b e´)	Whistle Stop
ALLMAN BROTHERS		
Little Martha	Open E	Eat A Peach
ALMEIDA, LAURINDO		
Intermezzo (from "A Love Story")	Drop-D	
Laura (from "Laura")	Drop-D	
The Bad And The Beautiful (Movie Theme)	Drop-D	
ANDERSON, MURIEL		
Nola	G6 (D G d g b e´)	*Fingerstyle Guitar Magazine*
AR BRAS, DAN		
Blood Of The Boat, The	Open G Capo II	Acoustic (LP)
Ten Years Already	D A d g a d´	Acoustic (LP)
ATKINS, CHET		
All Thumbs	Drop-D	Me And My Guitar
Black Mountain Rag	Open G	Stringin' Along

Explanation of Tunings Notation

1. Tunings are listed from the sixth string to the first (bass to treble). Pitches listed are at the nut, not at the capo position.

2. Letter names of tunings indicate the pitch and octave of each string:

    a) Lower case with a prime (d´, e´) indicates Middle C and the octave above it (c´ - b´). Most often these pitches are located on the first string--occasionally on the second;

    b) Lower case without a prime (a, b) indicates the octave below Middle C (c-b). Most often these pitches are located on the second, third, and fourth strings;

    c) Upper case (E, A) indicates the second octave below Middle C (C-B). Most often these pitches are located on the fifth and sixth strings;

    d) Upper case with a prime (A´, B´) indicates the third octave below Middle C (C´-B´). Most often these pitches are located on the sixth string.

3. Roman numerals (I, VII) indicate capo position. Partial capo indications are notated thusly: **Esus** = Capo II on strings 3, 4, 5; **A** = Capo II on strings 2, 3, 4; **E6sus** = Capo II on strings 2, 3, 4, 5.

4. Plus and minus markings ("+" and "-") indicate that the strings are tuned a number of half-steps above or below concert pitch. "Standard, -2" indicates Standard tuning, lowered two half-steps.

    Actual pitches: Standard, -1 = E^{b} A^{b} d^{b} g^{b} b^{b} e^{b}´; Standard, -2 = D G c f a d´; Standard, -3 = C$^{\#}$ F$^{\#}$ B e g$^{\#}$ c$^{\#}$´; Standard, -4 = C F B^{b} e^{b} g c´.

Artists' Tunes and Tunings

TITLE	TUNING	ALBUM

Chet Atkins, continued

Black Jack	Open D -2	Guitar Genius
Both Sides Now	D G d g b e´	Solid Gold '69, This Is Chet Atkins
Carnavalito	D G d g b e´	Class Guitar
Flop Eared Mule/Other Classics	C G d g b e´	Alone
Gavotte In D	Drop-D	Finger Style Guitar
Hawaiian Slack Key	Open G	Alone
Honolulu Blue	E A c# g b e´	Street Dreams, *Frets Magazine*, May '86
Just As I Am	C G d g b e´	Alone
Londonderry Air	Drop-D	Alone
Odd Folks Of Okracoke	Open D, +1	Now And Then
Smokey Mountain Lullaby	D G d g b e´	John Knowles *Fingerstyle Quarterly* Vol I, #1
Spanish Fandango	Open G	Alone, Frets Magazine Jan/Apr '86
Steeplechase Lane	D G d e b d´	Chet Atkins Picks on Jerry Reed
Vincent	Drop-D	Me And My Guitar
Yellow Bird	D G d g b e´	Class Guitar, This Is Chet Atkins

AUTEN, D.R.

Angela	Standard, -2	Acoustic Paintings

BAKER, DUCK

Note: "Salutation", originally released in 1987, will be re-released in 1996.

Duck estimates that 90% of his tunings for magazines, videos, and teaching tapes, or out-of-print recordings are Standard tuning; his next favorite is Drop-D. The keys for many of the tunes are noted in parentheses, i.e., (C) is the key of C Major. Some of the older recordings used Capo II.

Battle Cry of Freedom	Drop-D	American Traditional/ Fingerstyle Guitar Magazine Vol. I #5
Child of My Heart	Open G	*Fingerstyle Guitar* Magazine Vol. I #4

Explanation of Tunings Notation
1. Tunings are listed from the sixth string to the first (bass to treble). Pitches listed are at the nut, not at the capo position.
2. Letter names of tunings indicate the pitch and octave of each string:
   a) Lower case with a prime (d´, e´) indicates Middle C and the octave above it (c´ - b´). Most often these pitches are located on the first string--occasionally on the second;
   b) Lower case without a prime (a, b) indicates the octave below Middle C (c-b). Most often these pitches are located on the second, third, and fourth strings;
   c) Upper case (E, A) indicates the second octave below Middle C (C-B). Most often these pitches are located on the fifth and sixth strings;
   d) Upper case with a prime (A´, B´) indicates the third octave below Middle C (C´-B´). Most often these pitches are located on the sixth string.
3. Roman numerals (I, VII) indicate capo position. Partial capo indications are notated thusly: **Esus** = Capo II on strings 3, 4, 5; **A** = Capo II on strings 2, 3, 4; **E6sus** = Capo II on strings 2, 3, 4, 5.
4. Plus and minus markings ("+" and "-") indicate that the strings are tuned a number of half-steps above or below concert pitch. "Standard, -2" indicates Standard tuning, lowered two half-steps.
   Actual pitches: Standard, -1 = E♭ A♭ d♭ g♭ b♭ e♭´; Standard, -2 = D G c f a d´; Standard, -3 = C# F# B e g# c#´; Standard, -4 = C F B♭ e♭ g c´.

Artists' Tunes and Tunings

TITLE	TUNING	ALBUM
Dodder Bank, The	D G d g b e´ (G)	Opening The Eyes Of Love
Fanteladda/The Boys Of Ballisidare	E G d g b e´	Irish Reels, Jigs, Hornpipes & Airs
High On A Mountain/Poll Ha'penny	Open G Capo IV	The Moving Business
Hoggarth The Puss	D G d g c´ f´ (G minor)	(forthcoming release)
House Party Starting	E♭ A d g b e´ (C)	A Much Better Bridge (forthcoming)
I Saw Three Ships/ Good Christian Men Rejoice	D G d g b e´	The Salutation
Lament For Limerick	D G d g b e´	Irish Reels, Jigs, Hornpipes & Airs
Morgan Magan	Drop-D (A)	Irish Reels, Jigs, Hornpipes & Airs
Mother's Advice	Open D	American Traditional
Nottamun Town	D A d g a d´ Capo VII	The Moving Business
Pharoah's Army	D G d g b e´	Opening The Eyes Of Love
Salutation, The/In Bethlehem Town/ Lullay, Lullay	D A d g a d´ (D minor) Capo IV	The Salutation
Snow Dove	D A d g c f´ (D minor)	American Traditional
Tao Of Swing, The	Standard (C)	A Thousand Words
Trettondedagsmarschen	D G d g b e´	The Salutation

BAND, THE

Jemima Surrender	Drop-D Capo II	The Band

BARBEQUE BOB

California Blues	Open A, Capo I	Chocolate To The Bone
Diddle Da Diddle	Open D, Capo III	Chocolate To The Bone
Going Up The Country	Open A, Capo II	Chocolate To The Bone

BARBOSA-LIMA, CARLOS

Corcovado	Drop-D	Barbosa-Lima Plays The Music of Jobim & Gershwin
Desifinado	Drop-D	Barbosa-Lima Plays ....
One-Note Samba	Drop-D	Barbosa-Lima Plays ....

BASHO, ROBBIE

Variations On Easter	Open D	

BAUGHMAN, STEVE

A-Walking' I Will Go	C G d g c´ d´	Owner's Daughter
Iberian Gathering	E A A e a a	(forthcoming)
Planxty Bongwater	D G d g c´ d´	Owner's Daughter

Artists' Tunes and Tunings

TITLE	TUNING	ALBUM

BEAMER, KEOLA

Dancers In The Land Of Po	C G d g a d´ (C Ni'ihau/ Old Mauna Loa)	Wooden Boat
Don't You Want To Be My Baby?	C G d g b e´ (C Wahine)	Wooden Boat
E Ku'u Morning Dew	C G c g a d´ (C Ni'ihau/ Old Mauna Loa)	Moe 'Uhane Kika; Hawaiian...Masters
'Elepaio Slack Key	C F c g a f´	Wooden Boat
He Aloha No 'O Honolulu	C F c g c´ e´ (F Wahine)/ G´ C D G d g b d´ (8 str)-2	Wooden Boat
Kama Kani 'Olu 'Olu	D G d f# b d´	Hawaiian Slack Key Guitar
Kealia	C G e g a e´ (C Mauna Loa) Capo II	Wooden Boat
No Ke Ano Ahiahi	C G d g b e´ (C Wahine)	Wooden Boat
Papu Hinuhinu	C G d g b e´ (C Wahine)	
Po Mahina	C G d g b e´ (C Wahine)/ G´ C D G d g b d´ (8 str) -2	Wooden Boat
Shells	C G d g b e´ (C Wahine)	Wooden Boat
Wooden Boat	C G d g b e´ (C Wahine)	Wooden Boat

BEATLES, THE

Dear Prudence	Drop-D	White Album

BENSUSAN, PIERRE

Around The Day In Eighty Worlds	D A d g a d´ Capo II	Wu Wei
Doctor Graddus Ad Parnassum	C A d g a d´	
Gavottes	D G d g c´ d´	Pres de Paris
Pres de Paris/Reel	F G d g c´ f´ Capo IV	Early Pierre Bensusan
Si Bhig, Si Mhor	D A d g a d´	Musiques

BISHOP, STEPHEN

Rebecca	Standard	Ferrington Guitars Book/CD

Explanation of Tunings Notation
1. Tunings are listed from the sixth string to the first (bass to treble). Pitches listed are at the nut, not at the capo position.
2. Letter names of tunings indicate the pitch and octave of each string:
    a) Lower case with a prime (d´, e´) indicates Middle C and the octave above it (c´- b´). Most often these pitches are located on the first string--occasionally on the second;
    b) Lower case without a prime (a, b) indicates the octave below Middle C (c-b). Most often these pitches are located on the second, third, and fourth strings;
    c) Upper case (E, A) indicates the second octave below Middle C (C-B). Most often these pitches are located on the fifth and sixth strings;
    d) Upper case with a prime (A´, B´) indicates the third octave below Middle C (C´-B´). Most often these pitches are located on the sixth string.
3. Roman numerals (I, VII) indicate capo position. Partial capo indications are notated thusly: **Esus** = Capo II on strings 3, 4, 5; **A** = Capo II on strings 2, 3, 4; **E6sus** = Capo II on strings 2, 3, 4, 5.
4. Plus and minus markings ("+" and "-") indicate that the strings are tuned a number of half-steps above or below concert pitch. "Standard, -2" indicates Standard tuning, lowered two half-steps.
    Actual pitches: Standard, -1 = E♭ A♭ d♭ g♭ b♭ e♭´; Standard, -2 = D G c f a d´; Standard, -3 = C# F# B e g# c#´; Standard, -4 = C F B♭ e♭ g c´.

Artists' Tunes and Tunings

TITLE	TUNING	ALBUM

BLAKE, NORMAN

Spanish Fandango	Open G, -1 ($C^{\#}\ F^{\#}\ c^{\#}\ f^{\#}\ a^{\#}\ c^{\#\prime}$)	Back Home In Sulphur Springs

BLOCK, RORY

Crossroad Blues	Open G	High Healed Blues
Devil Got My Man	Open E	High Healed Blues
Kind Hearted	Open A Capo II	High Healed Blues
Walkin' Blues	Open A	High Healed Blues

BREAU, LENNY

NOTE: E A d g b e′ a′ Lenny normally played a 6-string in standard tuning, but also recorded with a 7-string guitar. The extra string was added on the treble side of the neck, tuned to a high a', a perfect fourth above the normal first string e'.

BROWN, GREG

If I Had Known	Drop-D	Down In There

BUCKINGHAM, LINDSAY

Never Going Back Again	C G d g b e′ (VI)	Rumours (Fleetwood Mac)

BUFFALO SPRINGFIELD

Pretty Girl Why	Drop-D	Last Time Around
Bluebird	D A d g b d′	Buffalo Springfield Again

CALE, J.J.

Danny's Song	Standard (E minor)	Ferrington Guitars Book/CD

CARTHY, MARTIN

NOTE: Favorite Martin Carthy tunings are: E A d e a e′, D A d e a e′, C G c d g d′, C D c d g a.

The Bedmaking	C G c d g a	Crown of Horn
Famous Flower Of Serving Men	D G d g c′ d′	
Molly Oxford	C G c d g d′	Out of the Cut
Peggy And The Soldier	D A d e a e′	Second Album
Sovay	D A d $c^{\#}$ a $c^{\#\prime}$ (Third string is tuned lower than fourth)	Brass Monkey
Willie's Lady	C G c d g g	Crown of Horn

CHASMAN, PAUL

Lonesome Fiddler	Drop-D	Just To Dance

Artists' Tunes and Tunings

TITLE	TUNING	ALBUM
Paul Chasman, continued		
Prokofiev Piano Sonata #7		Prokofiev Piano Sonata #7
Movements 1 & 2	Drop-D	
Movement 3	E G d g b e´	
Star Dust	Drop-C (C A d g b e´)	Real Songs
CHILLINGWORTH, SONNY		
Charmarita/Malasadas	D G d f$^{\#}$ b d´ (G Wahine)	Sonny Solo
Hi'ilawe	C G d g b d´ (C Wahine)	Sonny Solo
Ho'omalu Slack Key	Open G (Taro Patch)	Sonny Solo
Let Me Hear You Whisper	F G c g a e´ (Samoan C Mauna Loa) +2	Sonny Solo
Maori Brown Eyes	D G d e g d´ (C6 Mauna Loa)	Sonny Solo
Papakolea	D G d d g d´ (G Mauna Loa)	Sonny Solo
CLAPTON, ERIC		
Give Me Strength	Open E	461 Ocean Boulevard
Rollin' And Tumblin'	Open G	Unplugged
Running On Faith	Open G	Unplugged
Walkin' Blues	Open G	Unplugged
COCKBURN, BRUCE		
Cader Idris	E A d f$^{\#}$ b e´	Circles In The Stream
Foxglove	Open C (C G c g c´ e´) Capo II	Night Vision
God Bless The Children	Drop-D	Night Vision
Skylarking	E^{b} B^{b} d g b e´	Joy Will Find A Way
Sunwheel Dance	Open D	Sunwheel Dance
COLLINS, ALBERT		
Frosty	Open F minor (F c f a^{b} c´ f´) Capo IX	Frozen Alive
COLVIN, SHAWN		
Riding Shotgun Down The Avalanche	Drop-D Capo V	

Explanation of Tunings Notation

1. Tunings are listed from the sixth string to the first (bass to treble). Pitches listed are at the nut, not at the capo position.
2. Letter names of tunings indicate the pitch and octave of each string:
   a) Lower case with a prime (d´, e´) indicates Middle C and the octave above it (c´ - b´). Most often these pitches are located on the first string--occasionally on the second;
   b) Lower case without a prime (a, b) indicates the octave below Middle C (c-b). Most often these pitches are located on the second, third, and fourth strings;
   c) Upper case (E, A) indicates the second octave below Middle C (C-B). Most often these pitches are located on the fifth and sixth strings;
   d) Upper case with a prime (A´, B´) indicates the third octave below Middle C (C´-B´). Most often these pitches are located on the sixth string.
3. Roman numerals (I, VII) indicate capo position. Partial capo indications are notated thusly: **Esus** = Capo II on strings 3, 4, 5; **A** = Capo II on strings 2, 3, 4; **E6sus** = Capo II on strings 2, 3, 4, 5.
4. Plus and minus markings ("+" and "-") indicate that the strings are tuned a number of half-steps above or below concert pitch. "Standard, -2" indicates Standard tuning, lowered two half-steps.
   Actual pitches: Standard, -1 = E^{b} A^{b} d^{b} g^{b} b^{b} e^{b}´; Standard, -2 = D G c f a d´; Standard, -3 = C$^{\#}$ F$^{\#}$ B e g$^{\#}$ c$^{\#}$´; Standard, -4 = C F B^{b} e^{b} g c´.

Artists' Tunes and Tunings

TITLE	TUNING	ALBUM
COODER, RY		
Big Bad Bill Is Sweet William Now	Guitar 1: Open-D Capo V (Slide) Guitar 2: Drop-D Capo II	Jazz
Great Dream From Heaven	Drop-D	Into The Purple Valley
Happy Meeting In Glory	Drop-D, -2 (C F c f a d´)	Jazz
How Can A Poor Man Stand Such Times And Live	Open G	Show Time
Jesus On The Mainline	Open D, -2 (C G c e g c´)	Show Time
Vigilante Man	Open E	Into The Purple Valley
We Shall Be Happy	Drop-D Capo II	Jazz
COULON, MICHAEL		
Crossing Paths	Open D	Crossing Paths
Long Shadows	C G c g c´ e♭´	Crossing Paths
Path Of Fallen Leaves	D A d e a d´	Crossing Paths
Seven Devils Way	D A d g a d´	Crossing Paths
CROSBY, DAVID		
NOTE: Other Crosby tunings include C G d d a e´ and Standard		
Carry Me	Drop-D	Wind On The Water
Compass	E B d g a d´	American Dream (CSN&Y)
Deja Vu	E B d g a d´	Deja Vu (CSN&Y)
Guinnevere	E B d g a d´	Crosby, Stills And Nash
Laughing	D G d d a d´	If I Could Only Remember My Name
Music Is Love	D A d d a d´	If I Could Only Remember My Name
Traction In The Rain	A´ A d g b e´	If I Could Only Remember My Name
CROSBY, STILLS, & NASH		
In My Dreams	D A d d g c´	Crosby, Stills &Nash
Suite: Judy Blue Eyes	E E e e b e´	Crosby, Stills &Nash
CROSBY, STILLS, NASH & YOUNG		
Find The Cost Of Freedom	D A d g b d´, -2 (C G c f a c´)	So Far
Ohio	D A d g b d´	So Far
CUMMINGS, GLEN		
P.K.'s Blues	D A d g a d´	*Fingerstyle Guitar Magazine* #8

Artists' Tunes and Tunings

TITLE	TUNING	ALBUM

D'AGOSTINO, PEPPINO

Bella Donna	Open D	Sparks
Close To Heaven	F B^b d f c´ d´	Close To The Heart, *Fingerstyle Guitar Magazine* #10
Country Rain	e a d´ g´ b e´ *	Close To The Heart
Higher Connections	D A d g a d´	Close To The Heart
Mother's Tears	E B e g a d´	Close To The Heart
Pegasus	E B B f$^\#$ b e´	Sparks
Walk Away Renee	D A c$^\#$ e b c$^{\#}$´	Venus Over Venice

* e a d´ g´ b e´ is often called "Nashville Tuning." Four bass strings are strung with lighter strings and tuned one octave higher than Standard.

deGRASSI, ALEX

NOTE: Alex deGrassi has recorded considerable material with his three bass strings tuned E B e. Since this places considerable stress on the guitar, he suggests that guitarists consider tuning one whole-step lower for these tunings. For instance, E B e f$^\#$ b e´ becomes D A d e a d´.

All others on Southern Exposure are in standard tuning.

Alpine Medley	Open E	Turning: Turning Back
Causeway	E B e f$^\#$ b e´	Slow Circle
Children's Dance	Drop-D	Turning: Turning Back
Empty Room	D A d f$^\#$ b e´	Southern Exposure
Luther's Lullaby	E B e g c´ e´	Turning: Turning Back
McCormick	C A d g c´ f´	Altiplano
Midwestern Snow	E B e g$^\#$ b d$^{\#}$´	Slow Circle
Western	D A d g c´ e^{b}´	Southern Exposure
Window	E C e g c´ d´	Turning: Turning Back

DENVER, JOHN

Rocky Mountain High	Drop-D	Rocky Mountain High; Greatest Hits Vol I.
Poems, Prayers And Promises	Drop-D	Poems, Prayers And Promises

Explanation of Tunings Notation
1. Tunings are listed from the sixth string to the first (bass to treble). Pitches listed are at the nut, not at the capo position.
2. Letter names of tunings indicate the pitch and octave of each string:
    a) Lower case with a prime (d´, e´) indicates Middle C and the octave above it (c´ - b´). Most often these pitches are located on the first string--occasionally on the second;
    b) Lower case without a prime (a, b) indicates the octave below Middle C (c-b). Most often these pitches are located on the second, third, and fourth strings;
    c) Upper case (E, A) indicates the second octave below Middle C (C-B). Most often these pitches are located on the fifth and sixth strings;
    d) Upper case with a prime (A´, B´) indicates the third octave below Middle C (C´-B´). Most often these pitches are located on the sixth string.
3. Roman numerals (I, VII) indicate capo position. Partial capo indications are notated thusly: **Esus** = Capo II on strings 3, 4, 5; **A** = Capo II on strings 2, 3, 4; **E6sus** = Capo II on strings 2, 3, 4, 5.
4. Plus and minus markings ("+" and "-") indicate that the strings are tuned a number of half-steps above or below concert pitch. "Standard, -2" indicates Standard tuning, lowered two half-steps.
    Actual pitches: Standard, -1 = E^b A^b d^b g^b b^b e^b´; Standard, -2 = D G c f a d´; Standard, -3 = C$^\#$ F$^\#$ B e g$^\#$ c$^{\#}$´; Standard, -4 = C F B^b e^b g c´.

92

Artists' Tunes and Tunings

TITLE	TUNING	ALBUM
D'GARY		
E! Nama Inona Ny Anzaranao	E G e g g d´	Music From Madagascar
Kabary Boketra	Open D	Music From Madagascar
Manibili	E G A$^\#$ g a$^\#$ d´	Music From Madagascar
Tiambaly	D F d f f d´	Music From Madagascar
DOOBIE BROTHERS		
Black Water	D A d g b d´	Best of the Doobie Brothers
DOWLAND, JOHN		
Fantasia	E A d f$^\#$ b e´	*The Renaissance Guitar* (Noad)

DRAKE, NICK

NOTE: Common tunings for Nick Drake are: D A d g a f$^\#$, D A d g d´ g´, C G c f c´ e´, D G d d a d´, D A d g a d´ and D G d g a d´.

TITLE	TUNING	ALBUM
Fly	D A d g d´ g´	Fruit Tree
From The Morning	D A d g d´ f$^\#$´	Fruit Tree
Hanging On A Star	C G c f c´ e´	Fruit Tree
Pink Moon	D A d g d´ f$^\#$´	Fruit Tree
Place To Be	D A d g a f$^\#$´ Capo II	Pink Moon
Road	D G d d a d´ Capo III	Fruit Tree
DYKES, DOYLE		
Caleb's Report	D G d g b e´	Fingerstyle Guitar
Laguna Sand	D A d f$^\#$ b e´	Fingerstyle Guitar
Miss Haley's Music Box	Drop-D	Fingerstyle Guitar
White Rose For Heidi	C G d g b d´	Fingerstyle Guitar
EAGLES		
Bitter Creek	Open D-minor (D A d f a d´)	Desperado
EDELSEIN, ART		
"George Brabazon, Second Air"	Open G	Harp Music of Carolan for Solo Guitar
EDWARDS, KENNY		
Afternoon At George's	Drop-D	Ferrington Guitars Book/CD
EMMETT, RIK		
Midsummer's Daydream	Drop-D	Triumph (Stages)

Artists' Tunes and Tunings

TITLE	TUNING	ALBUM
EVANS, DAVE		
Hewlett	D G d g a d´	Solos In Open Tunings (Book)
Joly Mont	C G d g b e´	Fingerpicking Guitar Delights
Sheebeg An Sheemore	C G d g a d´	Solos In Open Tunings (Book)
FAHEY, JOHN		
Are You From Dixie?	Open E	I Remember Blind Joe Death
Auld Lang Syne	Open C (C G c g c´ e´)	Solos In Open Tunings (Book: S. Grossman Guitar Wkshp)
Desparate Man Blues	Open G (with unison G bass strings: G G d g b d´)	The Return Of The Repressed
Dance Of Death	Open G minor	Dance Of Death And Other Plantation Favorites
Dance Of The Inhabitants Of The Palace of King Phillip XIV of Spain	C c c g c´ e´	John Fahey, Vol. 2
Nightmare/Summertime	Open G minor Capo II	I Remember Blind Joe Death
Summertime	Open G minor, + 2 (E A e a c´ e´)	I Remember Blind Joe Death
Sunflower River Blues	Open C (C G c g c´ e´)	Fahey/Kottke/Lang
FINGER, PETER		
A Berryman's Tune	E A c# e a e´	Acoustic Rock Guitar
Colors Of The Night, The	E B e g a d´	The Colors Of The Night
Elf King, The	D G d g b♭ d´	Acoustic Rock Guitar
For Ladies I Couldn't Get	D A d f a d´	Acoustic Rock Guitar
For You	D A e g a d´	The Colors Of The Night
Magician's Apprentice, The	D A d f a d´	Acoustic Rock Guitar
Petermann's Polka	D A d g b d´	Acoustic Rock Guitar
Sinn Ohne Wörte	D A d g a d´	Innen Leben (Inner Life)
FINN, NEIL		
Melody	D G d g b e´	Ferrington Guitars Book/CD

Explanation of Tunings Notation
1. Tunings are listed from the sixth string to the first (bass to treble). Pitches listed are at the nut, not at the capo position.
2. Letter names of tunings indicate the pitch and octave of each string:
    a) Lower case with a prime (d´, e´) indicates Middle C and the octave above it (c´ - b´). Most often these pitches are located on the first string--occasionally on the second;
    b) Lower case without a prime (a, b) indicates the octave below Middle C (c-b). Most often these pitches are located on the second, third, and fourth strings;
    c) Upper case (E, A) indicates the second octave below Middle C (C-B). Most often these pitches are located on the fifth and sixth strings;
    d) Upper case with a prime (A´, B´) indicates the third octave below Middle C (C´-B´). Most often these pitches are located on the sixth string.
3. Roman numerals (I, VII) indicate capo position. Partial capo indications are notated thusly: **Esus** = Capo II on strings 3, 4, 5; **A** = Capo II on strings 2, 3, 4; **E6sus** = Capo II on strings 2, 3, 4, 5.
4. Plus and minus markings ("+" and "–") indicate that the strings are tuned a number of half-steps above or below concert pitch. "Standard, -2" indicates Standard tuning, lowered two half-steps.
    Actual pitches: Standard, -1 = E♭ A♭ d♭ g♭ b♭ e♭´; Standard, -2 = D G c f a d´; Standard, -3 = C# F# e g# c#´; Standard, -4 = C F B♭ e♭ g c´.

TITLE	TUNING	ALBUM

FLEETWOOD MAC

Never Going Back Again	C G d g b e´	Rumours (Fleetwood Mac)

FOGELBERG, DAN

Last To Know, The	Drop-D	Phoenix
Leader Of The Band	Standard Capo I	Innocent Age
Longer	Open G	Greatest Hits; Love Songs
Part Of The Plan	Open D	Souvenirs

FOSTER, RICK

Good King Wenceslas	Drop-D Capo II	
Prelude Of Joy	G6 (D G d g b e´)	*Fingerstyle Guitar Magazine* Vol. #4
Silent Night	D A d f# b e´	Season Of Joy
Sweet Hour Of Prayer	C G d g b e´	*Fingerstyle Guitar Magazine* Vol. #3

FRAMPTON, PETER

All I Want To Be	Open G	Comes Alive; Classics Vol. 12
Baby I Love Your Way	Standard	Comes Alive; Classics Vol. 12
One More Time	Open G	
Penny For Your Thoughts	Open D	Comes Alive
Wind Of Change	Open C (C G c g c´ e´) Capo II	Comes Alive; Shine On

GAUGHAN, DICK

Fair Flower Of Northumberland	Drop-D, Capo I	No More Forever
Jock O'Hazeldean	Standard, Capo III	No More Forever
MacCrimmon's Lament/Mistress Jamieson's Favourite	D G d g a d´ Capo VII	No More Forever

GERHARD, EDWARD

NOTE: Ed Gerhard mentions that he always tunes his 6-string guitar one half-step lower than standard pitch. He tunes his 12-string three half-steps lower than standard.

Blue Highway	B´ A d e a d´	Luna
Crow	E A d g a e´	Night Birds
French Lady, The	E G d g c´ d´	Night Birds
Gearhat	C G d g a d´	Luna
Handing Down, The	E A d e a e´	Luna/Windam Hill Guitar Sampler

95

Artists' Tunes and Tunings

TITLE	TUNING	ALBUM
Ed Garhard, continued		
Horses In The Rain	B´ G c f g c´	Luna
Lost Highway	E A c$^{\#}$ e a e´	Night Birds
Luna	C G c e^{b} b c´	Luna
No. 7	E A e e b e´	Night Birds
Si Bhig Si Mhor	D A d g b d´	Night Birds

GORE, JOE

These are listings of tunings adapted from those used by current rock groups. For further explanations, see Joe Gore's columns in the *Guitar Player* issues specified.

Tuning	*Guitar Player* Issue
E B B e b e´	*Guitar Player Magazine* (Dec. '92)
E A d a a e´	*Guitar Player* (Dec. '92)
B´ B´ d g b d´	*Guitar Player* (Dec. '92)
A(add9) (E A c$^{\#}$ e a b)	*Guitar Player* (Dec. '92)
E E c$^{\#}$ g b b	*Guitar Player* (Dec. '92)
F$^{\#}$ A d g a f$^{\#}$´	*Guitar Player* (Dec. '92)

Tunings with a Range of One Octave or Less:

G G d d g g	*Guitar Player* (Dec. '92)
G G c$^{\#}$ d g g	*Guitar Player* (Dec. '92)
G G d d a a	*Guitar Player* (Dec. '92)
G G d d f f	*Guitar Player* (Dec. '92)
G G c c f f	*Guitar Player* (Dec. '92)
G G c c e e	*Guitar Player* (Dec. '92)

GORKA, JOHN

Christmas Bells	Standard	Winter Solstice (Windham Hill)
Gypsy Life, The	Standard Capo V	Temporary Road

GRAHAM, DAVEY

Lord Inchiquin	E A d e a e´	Music of Ireland: Airs, Jigs...
Lord Mayo	E A d e a e´	Music Of Ireland: Airs, Jigs...

Explanation of Tunings Notation
1. Tunings are listed from the sixth string to the first (bass to treble). Pitches listed are at the nut, not at the capo position.
2. Letter names of tunings indicate the pitch and octave of each string:
   a) Lower case with a prime (d´, e´) indicates Middle C and the octave above it (c´ - b´). Most often these pitches are located on the first string--occasionally on the second;
   b) Lower case without a prime (a, b) indicates the octave below Middle C (c-b). Most often these pitches are located on the second, third, and fourth strings;
   c) Upper case (E, A) indicates the second octave below Middle C (C-B). Most often these pitches are located on the fifth and sixth strings;
   d) Upper case with a prime (A´, B´) indicates the third octave below Middle C (C´-B´). Most often these pitches are located on the sixth string.
3. Roman numerals (I, VII) indicate capo position. Partial capo indications are notated thusly: **Esus** = Capo II on strings 3, 4, 5; **A** = Capo II on strings 2, 3, 4; **E6sus** = Capo II on strings 2, 3, 4, 5.
4. Plus and minus markings ("+" and "-") indicate that the strings are tuned a number of half-steps above or below concert pitch. "Standard, -2" indicates Standard tuning, lowered two half-steps.
   Actual pitches: Standard, -1 = E^{b} A^{b} d^{b} g^{b} b^{b} e^{b}´; Standard, -2 = D G c f a d´; Standard, -3 = C$^{\#}$ F$^{\#}$ B e g$^{\#}$ c$^{\#}$´; Standard, -4 = C F B^{b} e^{b} g c´.

Artists' Tunes and Tunings

TITLE	TUNING	ALBUM
GRIFFITH, NANCI		
Ford Econoline	Drop-D	Lone Star State Of Mind
Ghost In The Music	D G d g a d´	Blue Moon
Lone Star State Of Mind	Drop-D	Lone Star State Of Mind
Love At The Five & Dime	Open G	Last Of The True Believers; Retrospective
GROSSMAN, STEFAN		
Blarney Pilgrim, The	G6 D G d g b e´	
House Carpenter	Open C (C G c g c´ e´)	Solos In Open Tunings (Book)
Jo And Her Daughters	Open G minor	Love, Devils And The Blues
La Rotta	E A d e a e´	Solos In Open Tunings (Book)
Woman From Donori	D A d g a d´	Snap A Little Owl

GULEZIAN, MICHAEL

NOTE: The treble courses of a 12-string (the e´ and b strings) are normally tuned in unison. Michael, however, at times tunes the two strings of each course (a pair of strings) to different pitches. This is notated with a slash between the two pitches: g^b/a^b, for example.

TITLE	TUNING	ALBUM
He Planned to Expand	D^b A^b d^b e^b a^b $d^{b´}$	The Dare of an Angel
House That Blocked Kansas, The	D A d g b d´	The Dare of an Angel
Mile High Country	C G d g a d´	The Dare of an Angel
Nothing Is Always Anything (12-string)	$B^{b´}$ F B^b f b^b c´	The Dare of an Angel
Tumbleweeb (12-string)	D^b G^b d^b f g^b/a^b $d^{b´}/e^{b´}$	The Dare of an Angel

GUTHRIE, ARLO

TITLE	TUNING	ALBUM
Highway In The Wind	D A d d a d´	Alice's Restaurant
Meditation (Wave Upon Wave)	D A d d a d´	Arlo
Motorcycle Song	E G d g b e´	Alice's Restaurant, Arlo

HAMMOND, JOHN

TITLE	TUNING	ALBUM
Drop Down Mama	Open A (E A e a $c^{#´}$ e´) (Open G, + 2)	John Hammond Live, Best of ...
Dust My Broom	Open E (Open D, +2)	John Hammond Live
One Kind Favor (12 String)	Drop-D, -2 (C G c f a d´)	John Hammond Live

HANSON, MARK

TITLE	TUNING	ALBUM
Boogie Woogie Jingle Bells	Drop-D	Yuletide Guitar
Devil's Dream	G6 (D G d g b e´)	Art of Solo Fingerpicking
Ryan Time (Again)	Drop-D	Music of Mark Hanson
Twin Sisters	D A d g a d´	Art of Solo Fingerpicking

TITLE	TUNING	ALBUM

HAVENS, RICHIE

Dolphins, The	Open D7 (D A d f$^\#$ a c´)	Richie Havens On Stage
Freedom	Open D, +1	Woodstock Video
From The Prison	Open Dm7 (D A d f a c´)	Richie Havens On Stage
God Bless The Child	Open D	Richie Havens On Stage
Handsome Johnny	Open D, -1	Woodstock Video
Just Like A Woman	Open D	Richie Havens On Stage
My Sweet Lord	Open D	Richie Havens On Stage

HEDGES, MICHAEL

About Face	D A d e a b	Taproot
Aerial Boundaries	C c d g a d´	Aerial Boundaries; Windham Hill Sampler '84
After The Goldrush	B´ F$^\#$ c$^\#$ d a d´	Aerial Boundaries
All Along The Watchtower	D A e e a a	Watching My Life Go By
Baby Toes	D A d g c´ d´	Breakfast In The Field
Bensusan	C G d g a c´	Aerial Boundaries
Buffalo Stance	B^{b}´ F c e^{b} f b^{b}	Taproot
Eleven Small Roaches	C G d g b d´	Breakfast In The Field
Funky Avocado	B´ A d g a d´	Breakfast.../Double Planet
Happy Couple, The	G B e f# a d´	Breakfast.../W.H. Sampler '82
Hot Type	A´ B e f$^\#$ a d´	Aerial Boundaries
I Carry Your Heart	B^{b}´ F c e^{b} f b^{b}	Taproot
Magic Farmer	C F c g a e´	Aerial Boundaries
Naked Stalk	D A d e a b	Taproot
Nomad Land	C G d g g g (three unison strings)	Taproot
Ragamuffin	D A d g a d´	Aerial Boundaries
Rootwitch	D A d g c´ c´	Taproot
Scenes	D A d e a b	Taproot
Silent Anticipations	D A d g c´ e´	Breakfast.../Double Planet

Explanation of Tunings Notation
1. Tunings are listed from the sixth string to the first (bass to treble). Pitches listed are at the nut, not at the capo position.
2. Letter names of tunings indicate the pitch and octave of each string:
    a) Lower case with a prime (d´, e´) indicates Middle C and the octave above it (c´ - b´). Most often these pitches are located on the first string--occasionally on the second;
    b) Lower case without a prime (a, b) indicates the octave below Middle C (c-b). Most often these pitches are located on the second, third, and fourth strings;
    c) Upper case (E, A) indicates the second octave below Middle C (C-B). Most often these pitches are located on the fifth and sixth strings;
    d) Upper case with a prime (A´, B´) indicates the third octave below Middle C (C´-B´). Most often these pitches are located on the sixth string.
3. Roman numerals (I, VII) indicate capo position. Partial capo indications are notated thusly: **Esus** = Capo II on strings 3, 4, 5; **A** = Capo II on strings 2, 3, 4; **E6sus** = Capo II on strings 2, 3, 4, 5.
4. Plus and minus markings ("+" and "-") indicate that the strings are tuned a number of half-steps above or below concert pitch. "Standard, -2" indicates Standard tuning, lowered two half-steps.
    Actual pitches: Standard, -1 = E^{b} A^{b} d^{b} g^{b} b^{b} e^{b}´; Standard, -2 = D G c f a d´; Standard, -3 = C$^\#$ F$^\#$ B e g$^\#$ c$^\#$´; Standard, -4 = C F B^{b} e^{b} g c´.

Artists' Tunes and Tunings

TITLE	TUNING	ALBUM
Michael Hedges, continued		
Spare Change	F A e g a d´	Aerial Boundaries/An Evening With Windham Hill Live
Two Days Old	D G d g b^b c´	Live On The Double Planet
Unexpected Visitor	C G e g b d´	Breakfast In The Field

HENDRIX, JIMI

TITLE	TUNING	ALBUM
Little Wing	Standard (lowered 1/2 step: E^b A^b D^b G^b B^b E^b)	Bold As Love
Purple Haze	Standard, -1	Woodstock Video
Star Spangled Banner	Standard, -1	Woodstock Video

HIDALGO, DAVID

TITLE	TUNING	ALBUM
Li'l King Of Everything	Open D	Ferrington Guitars Book/CD

HOOKER, JOHN LEE

TITLE	TUNING	ALBUM
If You've Never Been In Love	Standard, -2	Chill Out
Talkin' The Blues	Standard, -2	Chill Out
Terraplane Blues	Open D	Ultimate Collection 1948-1990
Woman On My Mind	Standard, -2	Chill Out

HOOPII, SOL

Hoopii tunings: E B d g$^#$ c$^{#}$´ e´; High Bass A (A c$^#$ e a c$^{#}$´ e´); C$^#$ minor (B d e g$^#$ c$^{#}$´ e´)

IAN, JANIS

TITLE	TUNING	ALBUM
This Train Still Runs	Drop-D Capo II on four bass strings	Breaking Silence

ILLENBERGER, RALF

TITLE	TUNING	ALBUM
Big Change	D B^b d g c´f´	Circle
Gemina	D B^b d g b^b d´	Circle
Nightflight	C A d g c´ e´	Circle

ISSACS, BARNEY

TITLE	TUNING	ALBUM
Maui Medley	Resonator: C E g a c´ e´ (G) 6 str: Open G (Taro Patch)	Hawaiian Touch With George Kuo; Hawaiian ... Masters

JAMES, SKIP

TITLE	TUNING	ALBUM
Hard Time Killing Floor	Open E minor (E B e g d e´)	Early Blues 1931

JANSCH, BERT

TITLE	TUNING	ALBUM
Blackwaterside	Drop-D Capo IV	The Songs of Bert Jansch (book)
First Time Ever I Saw Your Face, The	D A d g a d´	The Best Of Bert Jansch

Artists' Tunes and Tunings

TITLE	TUNING	ALBUM
Bert Jansch, continued		
Lost Love	F A d g b e' (standard with sixth string raised 1/2 step)	A Rare Conundrum
St. Fiacre	D A d g a d'	A Rare Conundrum
JENSEN, JAMES		
Bagdad Boogie	C G c g c' c'	
Snow Queen	C G c f# b d'	
JOHNSON, LONNIE		
Guitar Blues	G6 (D G d g b e')	Stepping on the Blues
Away Down In The Alley	G6 (D G d g b e')	Stepping on the Blues
JOHNSON, ROBERT		
Milkcow's Calf Blues	Open A	The Complete Recordings
Preaching Blues	Open E	The Complete Recordings
Traveling Riverside Blues	Open G Capo III	The Complete Recordings
Walking Blues	Open A Capo II	The Complete Recordings
JONES, WIZZ		
Country Comfort	Drop-D, Capo II	The Village Thing Tapes
First Girl I Loved, The	Open G	The Village Thing Tapes
JORDAN, STANLEY		
Touch of Blue	E A d g c' f'	One Night With Blue Note
JUBER, LAURENCE		
Age Of Rhythm, The	C G c g c' eb'	Between The Wars (Al Stewart)
Diminished Returns	Open G minor	LJ
Double Espresso	Open G	LJ
Feet On My Back Again	Open C (C G c g c' e')	LJ
Pass The Buck	D A d g a d'	LJ
KAAPANA, LEDWARD		
Whee Ha Swing	D G d f# b d'	Led Live Solo; Hawaiian...Masters

Explanation of Tunings Notation

1. Tunings are listed from the sixth string to the first (bass to treble). Pitches listed are at the nut, not at the capo position.
2. Letter names of tunings indicate the pitch and octave of each string:
    a) Lower case with a prime (d´, e´) indicates Middle C and the octave above it (c´ - b´). Most often these pitches are located on the first string--occasionally on the second;
    b) Lower case without a prime (a, b) indicates the octave below Middle C (c-b). Most often these pitches are located on the second, third, and fourth strings;
    c) Upper case (E, A) indicates the second octave below Middle C (C-B). Most often these pitches are located on the fifth and sixth strings;
    d) Upper case with a prime (A´, B´) indicates the third octave below Middle C (C´-B´). Most often these pitches are located on the sixth string.
3. Roman numerals (I, VII) indicate capo position. Partial capo indications are notated thusly: **Esus** = Capo II on strings 3, 4, 5; **A** = Capo II on strings 2, 3, 4; **E6sus** = Capo II on strings 2, 3, 4, 5.
4. Plus and minus markings ("+" and "-") indicate that the strings are tuned a number of half-steps above or below concert pitch. "Standard, -2" indicates Standard tuning, lowered two half-steps.
    Actual pitches: Standard, -1 = Eb Ab db gb bb eb'; Standard, -2 = D G c f a d'; Standard, -3 = C# F# B e g#c#'; Standard, -4 = C F Bb eb g c'.

Artists' Tunes and Tunings

TITLE	TUNING	ALBUM

KAHUMOKU, MOSES

Pohakuloa	Open G (Taro Patch)	Ho'okupu; Hawaiian ... Masters

KANE, RAY

NOTE: Ray Kane also uses Standard tuning, primarily on songs where he strums accompaniment for vocals.

Five Son Medley (Kealoha/Papkolea/ E Hulihuli Ho'i Mai/Mauna Loa/ Pua Makahala)	Open G (Taro Patch)	Punahele
Hi'ilawe	C G d g b e´ (C Wahine)	Master Of The Slack Key Guitar
Kila Kila Haleakala	E A e e f$^\#$c$^\#$´ (A Mauna Loa)	
La Paloma	Open G (Taro Patch)	Master Of The Slack Key Guitar
Nani Ho'omana'o	D A d f$^\#$ a c$^\#$´ (D Wahine)	Punahele
Poina Ole Slack Key	E A e e f$^\#$c$^\#$´ (A Mauna Loa)	
Punahele	D G d f$^\#$ b d´ (G Wahine)	Punahele, Master Of The Slack Key Guitar
Wa'ahila	Open G (Taro Patch) D G d f$^\#$ b d´ (G Wahine)	Master Of The Slack Key Guitar Wa'ahila

KAUKONEN, JORMA

Embryonic Journey	Drop-D	Surrealistic Pillow (Jefferson Airplane); Magic (Solo)
Water Song	Open G	Burgers (Hot Tuna)

KEAGGY, PHIL

Addison's Walk	D A d f$^\#$ b e´	Phil Keaggy Acoustic Solos (book)
Brother Jack	E B d g$^\#$ b d´	Phil Keaggy Acoustic Solos (book)
County Down	D A d g a d´	Phil Keaggy Acoustic Solos (book)
Fare Thee Well	E G$^\#$ e g$^\#$ b c´	Phil Keaggy Acoustic Solos (book)
Fragile Forest	E G$^\#$ e g$^\#$ b c´	Phil Keaggy Acoustic Solos (book)
Reunion, The	D A d g b d´	Phil Keaggy Acoustic Solos (book)

KINCAID, MATTHEW

Happy Birthday in D	Open D	*Acoustic Guitar Magazine* July '95

KIRTLEY, PAT

Amazing Grace	D A d g a d´	
B-Rod's Rag	Open G	Kentucky Guitar, Acoustic Guitar Music

Artists' Tunes and Tunings

TITLE	TUNING	ALBUM
Pat Kirtley, continued		
Daisy Goes A Dancing	D A d e a d´	Kentucky Guitar
In Church	Open G	Acoustic Guitar Music
Mountain Backstep	D A d d a d´	Acoustic Guitar Music
Sixteen Tons	E A d e a e´	Kentucky Guitar
Skye Boat Song	D A d g a d´	Irish Guitar
Steel Guitar Rag	E A d e a e´	Kentucky Guitar

Acoustic Guitar Music, recorded with Wendell Cornett in 1975, is currently out of print.

KNOWLES, JOHN

TITLE	TUNING	ALBUM
Blues Starter	E A c# g b e´	John Knowles *Fingerstyle Quarterly*, V.2, #2
Dark Moon	Drop-D (G minor)	*Fingerstyle Quarterly*, V.3, #4
Honolulu Blue	E A c# g b e´	*Fingerstyle Quarterly*, V.2, #2; *Fingerstyle Guitar* #10
Smoky Mountain Lullaby	D G d g b e´	*Fingerstyle Quarterly*, V.1, #1
Vincent	Drop-D Capo I	*Fingerstyle Quarterly*, V.1, #1

KOLM, MARK

TITLE	TUNING	ALBUM
Happy Birthday, Erin	C G d g a d´	*Acoustic Guitar Magazine* July '95

KOTANI, OZZIE

TITLE	TUNING	ALBUM
Ku'u Kika Kahiko	C G e g a e´ (C6 Mauna Loa)	Hawaiian ... Masters; Kani Ki Ho'Alu

KOTTKE, LEO

TITLE	TUNING	ALBUM
Arms Of Mary	Open G	Peculiaroso
Easter And The Sargasso Sea	Open G, -4 (B^b E^b B^b e^b g b^b)	20th Century Masters of Fingerstyle Guitar
Echoeing Gilewitz	Open D, -1	A Shout Toward Noon
First To Go	Drop-D, -1	A Shout Toward Noon
Ice Miner	Open G, Capo II	Mudlark
	Open G with 6th str down to G´ (G´ G d g b d´)	Fahey/Kottke/Lang
Jesu, Joy Of Man's Desiring	Open G, -1	6- And 12-String Guitar

Explanation of Tunings Notation
1. Tunings are listed from the sixth string to the first (bass to treble). Pitches listed are at the nut, not at the capo position.
2. Letter names of tunings indicate the pitch and octave of each string:
    a) Lower case with a prime (d´, e´) indicates Middle C and the octave above it (c´ - b´). Most often these pitches are located on the first string--occasionally on the second;
    b) Lower case without a prime (a, b) indicates the octave below Middle C (c-b). Most often these pitches are located on the second, third, and fourth strings;
    c) Upper case (E, A) indicates the second octave below Middle C (C-B). Most often these pitches are located on the fifth and sixth strings;
    d) Upper case with a prime (A´, B´) indicates the third octave below Middle C (C´-B´). Most often these pitches are located on the sixth string.
3. Roman numerals (I, VII) indicate capo position. Partial capo indications are notated thusly: **Esus** = Capo II on strings 3, 4, 5; **A** = Capo II on strings 2, 3, 4; **E6sus** = Capo II on strings 2, 3, 4, 5.
4. Plus and minus markings ("+" and "-") indicate that the strings are tuned a number of half-steps above or below concert pitch. "Standard, -2" indicates Standard tuning, lowered two half-steps.
    Actual pitches: Standard, -1 = E^b A^b d^b g^b b^{b}e^b´; Standard, -2 = D G c f a d´; Standard, -3 = C# F# B e g#c#´; Standard, -4 = C F B^b e^b g c´.

Artists' Tunes and Tunings

TITLE	TUNING	ALBUM
June Bug	Open G, -1	Mudlark
Little Martha	Open D, -1	A Shout Toward Noon
Louise	Drop-D, -3 (B′ F$^{\#}$ B e g$^{\#}$ c$^{\#}$′)	Greenhouse
Mona Ray	Drop-D	My Father's Face/Dreams And All That Stuff
Poor Boy	Open D, -3	Mudlark
Sailor's Grave On The Prairie	Open G, -4	6- And 12-String Guitar
San Antonio Rose/America, The Beautiful	Open G, -2	Dreams And All That Stuff
Three Walls And Bars	Drop D	Guitar Music
Times Twelve	Drop-D, -4	My Father's Face
Vaseline Machine Gun	Open G, -4	6- And 12-String Guitar
Wonderland By Night	Drop-D	Peculiaroso

KUO, GEORGE

Maui Medley	Resonator: C E g a c′ e′ (G) 6 str: Open G (Taro Patch)	Hawaiian Touch (with Barney Issacs); Hawaiian ... Masters

KWAN, LEONARD

Ke'ala's Mele	C G d g b d′ (C Wahine)	Ke'ala's Mele; Hawaiian ... Masters
Ki Hoalu	E A e e a e′	The Old Way
Pau Pilikia	C G c g a e′	Leonard Kwan

LANG, EDDIE

Guitar Blues	Drop-D	Stepping on the Blues

LANG, PETER

NOTE: Alternate tunings Peter Lang has used: Drop-D, Open D, Open G, D A d e a d′, D A d e c$^{\#}$ d′, D G d g b d′, D G d g b c$^{\#}$′, C G c g c′ e′, C G c g c′ d′, C E c g c′ e′, C G A g c′ e′, E A c$^{\#}$ e a c$^{\#}$′, E G$^{\#}$ B e b e′, G B d g b d′ (from *20th Century Finger-Style Guitar Masters*).

Adair's Song	Open G	The Thing At The Nursery Room Window
As I Lay Sleeping	Open D, -3	Fahey/Kottke/Lang
St. Charles Shuffle	C G c g c′ e′	Fahey/Kottke/Lang
Toth Song	C G c g c′ d′	Fahey/Kottke/Lang
V/The Connecticut Promissory Rag	C G A g c′ e′	Lycurgus

LED ZEPPELIN

Black Mountain Side	D A d g a d′	Led Zeppelin I
Bron-Y-Aur	C A c g c′ e′	Led Zeppelin III
Going To California	Open G	

TITLE	TUNING	ALBUM

LEE, ALBERT

Instrumental	Standard	Ferrington Guitars Book/CD

LEGG, ADRIAN

NOTE: British fingerstyle virtuoso Adrian Legg commonly retunes his guitar <u>during</u> a piece, with the help of banjo-style peg tuners. We have depicted these changes with a dash (-) between two pitches. For example: D A-G d g b d´ means the open fifth string (A) is tune down to a "G" during the course of the song. Adrian uses a high-strung guitar on occasion (four bass strings restrung and tuned one octave higher). He sometimes also uses two capos at once, "Brooklyn Blossom" for instance.

TITLE	TUNING	ALBUM
After The Gig	E G d g a d´; 4 bass strings Capo X	Guitar For Mortals
Brooklyn Blossom	Standard; Capo III; A-shape Capo V	Mrs. Crowe's Blue Waltz
Cajun Interlude	D A-G d g b d´ pegs section: D G d g b-a d-e reverts on final verse to: D G-A d g a-b e-d	Guitars & Other Cathedrals
Candle In Notre Dame, A	D G d g b e´	Guitar For Mortals
Coging's Glory	D A d g a d´	Guitar For Mortals
Gospel According To O. Henry	Open G to Open D D G-A d g-f$^{\#}$ b-a d´	Guitar For Mortals
Green Ballet II	E^{b}-D A d g b e´	Mrs. Crowe's Blue Waltz
Meditation Reprise	E A d f$^{\#}$ b e´, -2	Live
Midwest Sunday	D G d g b-a d´	Guitars & Other Cathedrals
Paddy Goes To Nashville	D A d f$^{\#}$-g a-b d´-e´	Mrs. Crowe's Blue Waltz
Piéta	E G d g b e´; 4 bass strings Capo V	Guitar For Mortals
Silent Night	D A d-e f$^{\#}$-g a-b d´	Wine, Women & Waltz
St. Mary's II (12 Str)	dD gG c´c f´f aa d´d´	Wine, Women & Waltz
Sweetheart	E-C G d g b e´	High Strung Tall Tales
Tune For Derroll	D A d-e f$^{\#}$-g a-b d´	Guitars & Other Cathedrals
Waltzin' With Jesus	Open D Capo II & lifted*	Guitar For Mortals

*Adrian Legg on occasion places an artificial nut under the strings, "lifting" the strings enough off the fingerboard to enable him to play slide guitar.

LINDLEY, DAVID

Look So Good	Open E	Win This Record

<u>Explanation of Tunings Notation</u>

1. Tunings are listed from the sixth string to the first (bass to treble). Pitches listed are at the nut, not at the capo position.

2. Letter names of tunings indicate the pitch and octave of each string:
       a) Lower case with a prime (d´, e´) indicates Middle C and the octave above it (c´- b´). Most often these pitches are located on the first string--occasionally on the second;
       b) Lower case without a prime (a, b) indicates the octave below Middle C (c-b). Most often these pitches are located on the second, third, and fourth strings;
       c) Upper case (E, A) indicates the second octave below Middle C (C-B). Most often these pitches are located on the fifth and sixth strings;
       d) Upper case with a prime (A´, B´) indicates the third octave below Middle C (C´-B´). Most often these pitches are located on the sixth string.

3. Roman numerals (I, VII) indicate capo position. Partial capo indications are notated thusly: **Esus** = Capo II on strings 3, 4, 5; **A** = Capo II on strings 2, 3, 4; **E6sus** = Capo II on strings 2, 3, 4, 5.

4. Plus and minus markings ("+" and "-") indicate that the strings are tuned a number of half-steps above or below concert pitch. "Standard, -2" indicates Standard tuning, lowered two half-steps.
       Actual pitches: Standard, -1 = E^{b} A^{b} d^{b} g^{b} b^{b} e^{b}´; Standard, -2 = D G c f a d´; Standard, -3 = C$^{\#}$ F$^{\#}$ B e g$^{\#}$ c$^{\#}$´; Standard, -4 = C F B^{b} e^{b} g c´.

Artists' Tunes and Tunings

TITLE	TUNING	ALBUM

LOGGINS, KENNY

Real Thing, The	Open G (with C bass: C G d g b d´)	Leap Of Faith

LOWRY, GARY

Blessed Assurance	C G d g b e´	*Fingerstyle Guitar Magazine #9*

MacLEAN, DOUGIE

Caledonia	Open D Capo II	Collection
Little Ones Walk On	D A d g a d´ Capo I	Whitewash
Ready for the Storm	Open G Capo I	Collection
Turning Away	Open D minor Capo IV	Collection

MARTYN, JOHN

NOTE: John Martyn also uses "Cello Tuning": C F c c g d´

Fairy Tale Lullaby	Open D	

MARX, RICHARD

Flame of Love, The	Open D minor (D A d f a d´)	

McDOWELL, MISSISSIPPI FRED

Tunings: Open E, Open A , Standard

McCASLIN, MARY

Circle Of Friends	Open D	Way Out West
Let It Be Me	D G d g b^b d´	Way Out West
Northfield	Open C (C G c g c´ e´)	Way Out West
Way Out West	E A d f$^{\#}$ b e´	Way Out West

McLEAN, DON

Castles In The Air	Drop-D	Tapestry
Three Flights Up	Drop-D	Tapestry

McMEEN, EL

Carolan's Farewell To Music	C G d g a d´	Soul and Spirit
Carolan's Dream	C G d g a d´	Solo Guitar Serenade

McTELL, RALPH

Autumn	Drop-D (Lowered one whole-step: C G c f a d')	The Guitar & Songs Of Ralph McTell (book)

Artists' Tunes and Tunings

TITLE	TUNING	ALBUM
Ralph McTell, continued		
Hands Of Joseph	Drop-D	The Guitar & Songs Of...
Tequila Sunset	Drop-D	The Guitar & Songs Of...
Water Of Dreams	Open D	The Guitar & Songs Of...
METHENY, PAT		
Phase Dance	Nashville Tuning (e a d′ g′ b e′: four bass strings one octave higher than normal)	Pat Metheny Group Travels Live
MILLER, DALE		
Were You There	Open D	Both of Me
MILLER, JOE		
Wedding Music	Open D Capo I or Open E^b (E^b B^b e^b g b^b e^b′)	Semi-Traditional Guitar Solos
MITCHELL, JONI		
A Bird That Whistles	Open C Capo II	Chalk Mark In A Rainstorm
Amelia	Open D Open D, -2 (C G c e c′ e′)	Shadows And Light; Hejira
Both Sides Now	Open D Capo IV	Clouds
Cold Blue Steel And Sweet Fire	Open G (with C bass: C G d g b d′)	For The Roses
Coyote	Open D, -2 (C G c e c′ e′)	Hejira
I Don't Know Where I Stand	F F c g a c′ (unison 5th & 6th) Capo III	Clouds
Morning Morgantown	Open G	Ladies Of The Canyon
That Song About The Midway	D A d e a e′ Capo II	Clouds
This Flight Tonight	Open G + 1 (6th lowered to A^b′: A^b′ A^b e^b a^b c′ e^b′)	Blue
MIZE, BILL		
Amaranth	C G c g c′ d′	Tender Explorations

<u>**Explanation of Tunings Notation**</u>
1. Tunings are listed from the sixth string to the first (bass to treble). Pitches listed are at the nut, not at the capo position.
2. Letter names of tunings indicate the pitch and octave of each string:
    a) Lower case with a prime (d′, e′) indicates Middle C and the octave above it (c′ - b′). Most often these pitches are located on the first string--occasionally on the second;
    b) Lower case without a prime (a, b) indicates the octave below Middle C (c-b). Most often these pitches are located on the second, third, and fourth strings;
    c) Upper case (E, A) indicates the second octave below Middle C (C-B). Most often these pitches are located on the fifth and sixth strings;
    d) Upper case with a prime (A′, B′) indicates the third octave below Middle C (C′-B′). Most often these pitches are located on the sixth string.
3. Roman numerals (I, VII) indicate capo position. Partial capo indications are notated thusly: **Esus** = Capo II on strings 3, 4, 5; **A** = Capo II on strings 2, 3, 4; **E6sus** = Capo II on strings 2, 3, 4, 5.
4. Plus and minus markings ("+" and "-") indicate that the strings are tuned a number of half-steps above or below concert pitch. "Standard, -2" indicates Standard tuning, lowered two half-steps.
    Actual pitches: Standard, -1 = E^b A^b d^b g^b b^b e^b′; Standard, -2 = D G c f a d′; Standard, -3 = C$^\#$ F$^\#$ B e g$^\#$ c$^\#$′; Standard, -4 = C F B^b e^b g c′.

Artists' Tunes and Tunings

TITLE	TUNING	ALBUM
Freefall	D A d e a d´	Tender Explorations
Miasmia	D A d f c´ d´	Tender Explorations
Rose In A Fire, A	D G d g b e´	Tender Explorations
Silver Plume Waltz	D A d g a d´ Capo II	Sugarlands
Tender Explorations	D A d g a d´	Tender Explorations

MOORE, TRACY

Bob Takes His Truck To The Dump (12 Str)	D G d g b c´, -2	A Peculiar Point Of Balance
Dilettante Sidestep	Open G, -1	Skypiece
Highland Drive (12 String)	C G d g b c´ (capo over all strings except bass pair on 12-String), -2	A Peculiar Point Of Balance
I Love My Attitude Problem (12 String)	C G c g c´ d´ Capo II, -1	A Peculiar Point Of Balance
Peculiar Point Of Balance, A (12 String)	D G d g b c´, -2	A Peculiar Point Of Balance
Skypiece (12 String)	D G d g b c´, -3	Skypiece
Swanee River Boogie (12 String)	Open C (C G c g c´ e´) Skypiece: -1 Peculiar Pt: -3	Skypiece, A Peculiar Point...

MUDARRA

Fantasia	E A D f$^\#$ b e´	*The Renaissance Guitar* (Noad)

NEIL, FRED

Dolphins	Drop-D	Fred Neil

NIEHOUSE, EILEEN

All Tunes On Album:	D A d g a d´	Mad Grace

NIRVANA

Lithium	Open D	Nevermind

O'CONNER, MARK

Dixie Breakdown	Standard, -1	Retrospective

OWENS, BUCK

Buckaroo	Standard, -1	Buck Owens Collection 1959-1990

PAGE, JIMMY

Black Mountain Side	D A d g a d´	Led Zeppelin I
Bron-Y-Aur	C A c g c´ e´	Led Zeppelin III

Artists' Tunes and Tunings

TITLE	TUNING	ALBUM

PAHINUI, CYRIL

Hanauma Bay (12 String)	C G e g c´ e´	6 & 12 String Slack Key
Lullaby For Pops	D A d f$^\#$ b e´	6 & 12 String Slack Key
Moloka'i-nui-a-Hina (12 String)	D A d f$^\#$ b e´	6 & 12 String Slack Key
Noenoe (12 String)	C G e g a e´ (Mauna Loa)	6 & 12 String Slack Key
Young Street Blues	Open G (Taro Patch)	6 & 12 String Slack Key

PAHINUI, GABBY

Title	Tuning	Album
No Ke Ano Ahiahi	C G e g a e´, -3 (C Mauna Loa)	An Island Heritage
	C G e g a e´ (C Mauna Loa)	The Gabby Pahinui Hawaiian Band Vol 2.

ERIC PARK

Title	Tuning	Album
Healthcliff's Last Ride	G minor (D G d g b^b d´	Woodlark
Hummingbird	G Maj7 (D G d f$^\#$ b d´)	Woodlark
Passing Breeze	C7 + 9 (C G c g b^b d´)	Woodlark

PARKENING, CHRISTOPHER

Title	Tuning	Album
Prelude No. 1	Drop-D	Parkening Plays Bach
Sheep May Safely Graze	C G d g b e´	Parkening Plays Bach

PEARL JAM

Title	Tuning	Album
Deep	E A c$^\#$ e a e´	Ten
Even Flow	Open D	Ten
Garden	Drop-D	Ten
Oceans	Open D	Ten

PERLMAN, KEN

Title	Tuning	Album
Napoleon Crossing The Rhine	Drop-D	Fingerpicking Fiddle Tunes (book)
Sheebeg Agus Sheemore	Drop-D	Fingerpicking Fiddle Tunes (book)

PENTANGLE

Title	Tuning	Album
Reynardine	Drop D	So Early In The Spring

Explanation of Tunings Notation

1. Tunings are listed from the sixth string to the first (bass to treble). Pitches listed are at the nut, not at the capo position.
2. Letter names of tunings indicate the pitch and octave of each string:
    a) Lower case with a prime (d´, e´) indicates Middle C and the octave above it (c´ - b´). Most often these pitches are located on the first string--occasionally on the second;
    b) Lower case without a prime (a, b) indicates the octave below Middle C (c-b). Most often these pitches are located on the second, third, and fourth strings;
    c) Upper case (E, A) indicates the second octave below Middle C (C-B). Most often these pitches are located on the fifth and sixth strings;
    d) Upper case with a prime (A´, B´) indicates the third octave below Middle C (C´-B´). Most often these pitches are located on the sixth string.
3. Roman numerals (I, VII) indicate capo position. Partial capo indications are notated thusly: **Esus** = Capo II on strings 3, 4, 5; **A** = Capo II on strings 2, 3, 4; **E6sus** = Capo II on strings 2, 3, 4, 5.
4. Plus and minus markings ("+" and "–") indicate that the strings are tuned a number of half-steps above or below concert pitch. "Standard, -2" indicates Standard tuning, lowered two half-steps.
    Actual pitches: Standard, -1 = E^b A^b d^b g^b b^b e$^{b´}$; Standard, -2 = D G c f a d´; Standard, -3 = C$^\#$ F$^\#$ B e g$^\#$ c$^{\#´}$; Standard, -4 = C F B^b e^b g c´.

Artists' Tunes and Tunings

TITLE	TUNING	ALBUM

PETTAWAY, AL

TITLE	TUNING	ALBUM
Chesapeake	D A d g a d´	The Waters And The Wild
Magik	D A d g a d´ Capo V	Whispering Stones
(A) New Dawn	Open G Capo II	Whispering Stones
Sidh Beag, Sidh Mor	Drop-D Capo II	Whispering Stones
Songline To Skye	C G c g c´ c´	Midsummer Moon
Whispering Stones	C G c g c´ e$^{b´}$	Whispering Stones

PINK FLOYD

TITLE	TUNING	ALBUM
Wish You Were Here (12-String)	Standard	

POWELL, BADEN

TITLE	TUNING	ALBUM
Deve Ser Amor	Standard	*Frets Magazine,* Jan, '87

PROCTOR, CHRIS

Note: Chris Proctor often uses the "Third-Hand Capo," an elastic-band style capo with individual cams, allowing different combinations of strings to be fretted by the capo.

TITLE	TUNING	ALBUM
A Trip To Jackie's House	Esus4 (Third Hand)	The Delicate Dance
California Dreaming	Open G minor	Steel String Stories
Canyonlands	D A d g b d´	Runoff
Emperor's Choice, The	E A c$^{#}$ e b e´	His Journey Home
From LA To Zaire	C G d g b d´	Steel String Stories
Sad Pig Dance, The	C G d g b^{b} d´	The Delicate Dance
Swept Away	C G d g b^{b} d´	The Delicate Dance

PURE PRAIRIE LEAGUE

TITLE	TUNING	ALBUM
Angel	Open G Capo I	

RAITT, BONNIE

TITLE	TUNING	ALBUM
Dimming Of The Day	Standard Capo I	Longing In Their Hearts
Shadow Of Doubt	Open G, +1 (E^{b} A^{b} e^{b} a^{b} c´ e$^{b´}$)	Longing In Their Hearts
That Song About The Midway	Drop-D Capo II	Streetlights
Thing Called Love	Open A (E A e a c$^{#´}$ e´)	Nick Of Time
Write Me A Few Of Your Lines	Open A (E A e a c$^{#´}$ e´)	Takin' My Time

RAMSEY, WILLIS ALAN

TITLE	TUNING	ALBUM
Muskrat Love	Standard (E)	Willis Alan Ramsey
Satin Shoes	Open G	Willis Alan Ramsey
Watermelon Man	Open E	Willis Alan Ramsey

Artists' Tunes and Tunings

TITLE	TUNING	ALBUM

REED, PRESTON

Blue Vertigo	A′ E d g b e′	Blue Vertigo
Border Towns	C G d g a d′	Border Towns, Metal
Chattanooga (Slide)	B′ G d g a d′	Metal
Flatonia	C G d g b e′	Instrument Landing, Metal
Overture (For Lily) (12 String)	Open D -3	Metal
Slap Funk	C G d g b e′	Blue Vertigo/Metal
Tribes	C G d g g d′	Metal, The Guitar of Preston Reed Video

REID, HARVEY

Harvey's tunings are very creative. A bit of explanation is required to make our notations understandable:

"Standard, -2" indicates Standard tuning, but lowered two half-steps. See chart below for actual pitches to use with chromatic tuners.

Harvey uses partial capos. For example, Esus means third, fourth, and fifth strings are capoed at the 2nd fret. See chart below for further examples.

Harvey sometimes uses two capos at once. For example, *To The Western Wind* has the markings "II + Esus IV" This indicates that Harvey uses two capos: a full capo at the second fret (II), and (+) a partial capo on the third, fourth and fifth strings (Esus) at the 4th fret (IV).

Albatross (Resonator Guitar)	Open A^b ($E^b A^b e^b a^b c′ e^b$)	all strings Capo I except open 2nd	Nothin' But Guitar; Solo Guitar Sketchbook
Annie Laurie	Drop-D	no capo	Chestnuts
Circles	Drop-D, -1	II	Circles
Für Elise	Open E^b ($E^b B^b e^b g^b b^b e^b$))	I for 5 str.; open 3rd	Solo Guitar Sketchbook
Oh Marie	E B e e b e′	Esus II	Circles
Oh Susannah (12 String)	$C^\# E B e g^\# c^{\#′}$	Top five strings, II	Steel Drivin' Man
Scarborough Fair	Open D^b	all str. I except open 3rd	Chestnuts

Explanation of Tunings Notation

1. Tunings are listed from the sixth string to the first (bass to treble). Pitches listed are at the nut, not at the capo position.
2. Letter names of tunings indicate the pitch and octave of each string:
   a) Lower case with a prime (d′, e′) indicates Middle C and the octave above it (c′ - b′). Most often these pitches are located on the first string--occasionally on the second;
   b) Lower case without a prime (a, b) indicates the octave below Middle C (c-b). Most often these pitches are located on the second, third, and fourth strings;
   c) Upper case (E, A) indicates the second octave below Middle C (C-B). Most often these pitches are located on the fifth and sixth strings;
   d) Upper case with a prime (A′, B′) indicates the third octave below Middle C (C′-B′). Most often these pitches are located on the sixth string.
3. Roman numerals (I, VII) indicate capo position. Partial capo indications are notated thusly: **Esus** = Capo II on strings 3, 4, 5; **A** = Capo II on strings 2, 3, 4; **E6sus** = Capo II on strings 2, 3, 4, 5.
4. Plus and minus markings ("+" and "-") indicate that the strings are tuned a number of half-steps above or below concert pitch. "Standard, -2" indicates Standard tuning, lowered two half-steps.
   Actual pitches: Standard, -1 = $E^b A^b d^b g^b b^b e^{b′}$; Standard, -2 = D G c f a d′; Standard, -3 = $C^\# F^\# B e g^\# c^{\#′}$; Standard, -4 = C F $B^b e^b$ g c′.

Artists' Tunes and Tunings

TITLE	TUNING	ALBUM

RENBOURN, JOHN

TITLE	TUNING	ALBUM
Bicycle Tune	E A d f$^\#$ b e´ (Lute tuning)	The Hermit
Bouree I & II	C G c g c´ f´	Black Balloon
Cherry	D G d g b e´	The Three Kingdoms, Jazz Tinge
Country Blues	E A d g a e´	Faro Annie
Estampie	F$^\#$ A c$^\#$ f$^\#$ a c$^\#$´	(forthcoming)
Faro Anne	E A d g a e´	Faro Anne
Goat Island	D A e g b e´	The Hermit
Hermit, The	Drop-D	The Hermit
John's Tune	D G d g b e´	The Hermit
I Love My Love	E G$^\#$ c$^\#$ f$^\#$ b e´	Enchanted Garden
Judentanz	E B B f$^\#$ b e´	A Maid In Bedlam (J.R. Group)
Le Tambourin	D G d g b b^b d´	Enchanted Garden
Maid On The Shore, The	E G$^\#$ c$^\#$ f$^\#$ b e´	Enchanted Garden
Merrily Kissed The Quaker	E A d e a e´	Frets Magazine (Jan. '89)
Mist Covered Mountains Of Home	Open G minor	Black Balloon
My Sweet Potato	Drop-D	Sir John Alot
Nine Maidens, The	Open G minor	The Nine Maidens
Orphan, The/Tarboulton	Open G minor	Black Balloon
Palermo Snow	D A d g b^b e´	(forthcoming)
Pelican	D A d e a d´	Black Balloon
Sidi Brahim	F B^b c g c´ f´	Enchanted Garden
Sigoniatanz	E B B f$^\#$ b e´	Maid In Bedlam
South Wind	D A d g b d´	Guitar Player (Sep. '92)/ Ship Of Fools
Sweet Potato	Drop-D	Sir John Alot

NOTE: John Renbourn suggested we group his tunings according to their closest keys. The following list shows the key or keys most likely to ge used for each of his tunings.

Key	Tunings
E	E A d f$^\#$ b e´
B	E A d f$^\#$ b e´, E G$^\#$ c$^\#$ f$^\#$ b e´, E B B f$^\#$ b e´
A	E A d g a e´, E A d e a e´, E A e f$^\#$ a d´, D A e g b e´
D	D A d g b e´, D A d e a d´, D A d g a d´, D A d f$^\#$ a d´, D A d g b^b d´
G	D G d g b e´, D G d g b d´, D G d g b^b d´, D G d g c´ d´, G B^b d g b^b d´
C	C G c g c f´, C B^b c f b^b f´, F B^b c g c´ f´

Artists' Tunes and Tunings

TITLE	TUNING	ALBUM

REUSSNER, BREVE

Anecdota	Drop-D	Song Without Words

ROGERS, ROY

Bad Situation	Open E	Slide Of Hand
Change Of The Season	Open G	Slide Of Hand
Slide Of Hand	Open G, +1	Slide Of Hand
Stones In My Passway	Open D	Slide Of Hand
Work Hard For The Money	Open A	Slide Of Hand

ROLLING STONES

Keith Richard often tunes to Open G tuning, and removes the bass string. The tuning (fifth string to first) is: G d g b d´

RUSH, TOM

No Regrets	Open C, -2 ($B^{b´}$ F B^b f b^b d´)	Circle Game
Rockport Sunday	Open C, -2 ($B^{b´}$ F B^b f b^b d´)	Circle Game

SCHOENBERG, ERIC

Devrah's Delight	D G d g c´ d´	Steel Strings
Green Fields of Canada, The/ Sleepy Maggie	F G d g c´ d´	Acoustic Guitar
Planxty Irwin/Wise Maid	Open G	Acoustic Guitar
Rights Of Man	D A d g a d´	Steel Strings

SCHORER, DYLAN

Tunings used by Dylan Schorer: Open D, Open G, D A d g a d´, D E d g a d´, C G e^b g c´ d´, C G d g c´ d´, Drop-D plus A II (partial capo A major); E B d $f^\#$ b d´.

SCRUGGS, RANDY

Both Sides Now	Open G	Will the Circle Be Unbroken
Amazing Grace	Open G	Will the Circle Be Unbroken II

<u>**Explanation of Tunings Notation**</u>

1. Tunings are listed from the sixth string to the first (bass to treble). Pitches listed are at the nut, not at the capo position.
2. Letter names of tunings indicate the pitch and octave of each string:
    a) Lower case with a prime (d´, e´) indicates Middle C and the octave above it (c´ - b´). Most often these pitches are located on the first string--occasionally on the second;
    b) Lower case without a prime (a, b) indicates the octave below Middle C (c-b). Most often these pitches are located on the second, third, and fourth strings;
    c) Upper case (E, A) indicates the second octave below Middle C (C-B). Most often these pitches are located on the fifth and sixth strings;
    d) Upper case with a prime (A´, B´) indicates the third octave below Middle C (C´-B´). Most often these pitches are located on the sixth string.
3. Roman numerals (I, VII) indicate capo position. Partial capo indications are notated thusly: **Esus** = Capo II on strings 3, 4, 5; **A** = Capo II on strings 2, 3, 4; **E6sus** = Capo II on strings 2, 3, 4, 5.
4. Plus and minus markings ("+" and "-") indicate that the strings are tuned a number of half-steps above or below concert pitch. "Standard, -2" indicates Standard tuning, lowered two half-steps.
    Actual pitches: Standard, -1 = E^b A^b d^b g^b b^b $e^{b´}$; Standard, -2 = D G c f a d´; Standard, -3 = $C^\#$ $F^\#$ B e $g^\#$ $c^{\#´}$; Standard, -4 = C F B^b e^b g c´.

Artists' Tunes and Tunings

TITLE	TUNING	ALBUM

SEEGER, PETE

Living In The Country	Drop-D	Greatest Hits

SETE, BOLA

Let Go	Drop-D	Ocean
Vira Mundo Penba	Drop-D	Ocean

SIMON, PAUL

Anji	Standard Capo III	Sounds of Silence
Late Great Johnny Ace	Standard, -2	Simon & Garfunkel--Concert in Central Park
Peace Like a River	Standard, -2	Paul Simon
Scarborough Fair	Standard Capo VII	Parsley, Sage, Rosemary & Thyme

SIMPSON, MARTIN

Admiral Benbow	D A d g a d´ Capo V	A Cut Above
Banks Of The Bann	Drop-D	Leaves Of Life
Bantry Girl's Lament	Drop-D -7 (baritone guitar tuned 3 1/2 steps below standard, or G´ D G c e a)	Leaves Of Life
Bob's Song	C G c g c´ d´ Capo II	When I Was On Horseback
Bonny At Morn	D A d f a d´	When I Was On Horseback
Bonnie George Campbell	C F c g c´ d´	Leaves Of Life
Charlie's Boogie	Open G	Nobody's Fault But Mine; Acoustic Guitar of...(book)
Davy Lowston	D G d g c´ d´	A Cut Above (June Tabor)
Fair Flower Of Northumberland, The	Drop-D	Leaves Of Life
Fanny Power	C G c g c´ d´	Music Of Ireland
Flash Company	D A d g a d´ Capo VII	A Cut Above
Flower Of Sweet Erin The Green	D G d g c´ d´ Capo II	When I Was On Horseback
Garryowen	D A d g a d´ Capo III	When I Was On Horseback
Golden Vanity	Open D	Golden Vanity
Granuaile	C G c g c´ d´	When I Was On Horseback
Green Linnet/Grinning In Your Face	C G c g c´ g´	Martin Simpson: The Collection
Greenfields Of America	Open C (C G c g c´ e´)	Leaves Of Life
Hard Time Killing Floor	Open D^7 (D A d g a c´)	Nobody's Fault But Mine
Heather Down The Moor	D A d g a d´	A Cut Above
Icarus	C G c g c´ d´ Capo III	Red Roses

Artists' Tunes and Tunings

TITLE	TUNING	ALBUM
Martin Simpson, continued		
Kindness Of Strangers	D G d g c´ d´ Capo III	Band Of Angels
Leaves Of Life	D A d g a c´	Leaves Of Life
Lilith	C G d g a d´	Band Of Angels
Lucy Wan	D A d g a c´	Leaves Of Life
Masters Of War	Open C minor (C G c g c´ e^b´)	Martin Simpson: The Collection
Mermaid, The	C G c f a d´	Red Roses
Raglan Road	B^b´ F B^b f b^b c´	Band Of Angels
Roadkill	D A d g a c´	Smoke And Mirrors
Spare Change	D G d g a d´ Capo IV	Red Roses
We Were All Heroes	C G c f c´ d´	Red Roses
Wondrous Love	D A d g a d´ to D A d g a c´	A Closer Walk With Thee
Young Man	C G c f c´ d´	When I Was On Horseback
SMASHING PUMPKINS		
Mayonnaise	Guitar 1: E^b B^b B^b g^b b^b d´ Guitar 2: Standard, -1 Capo IV	Siamese Dreams
Today	Standard Capo I	Siamese Dreams
SMITH, DOUG		
Barbara's Valentine	D A d g a e´	Dayparts:Romance
Crest Of The Revolution	E A d g b c´	Order Of Magnitude
Hammerhead	D G d g b^b c´	Labyrinth
Lost In The Here And Now	D G d g a e´ Capo II	Labyrinth
Order Of Magnitude	D G d g a d´ Capo III	Order Of Magnitude
Rites Of Passage	F G d g b^b d´	Order Of Magnitude
Shadowcasting	C A d g b e´	Labyrinth
When The Walls Fell	Drop-D	Labyrinth
SMITHER, CHRIS		
Mail Order Mystics	Open D	Happier Blue

Explanation of Tunings Notation
1. Tunings are listed from the sixth string to the first (bass to treble). Pitches listed are at the nut, not at the capo position.
2. Letter names of tunings indicate the pitch and octave of each string:
    a) Lower case with a prime (d´, e´) indicates Middle C and the octave above it (c´ - b´). Most often these pitches are located on the first string--occasionally on the second;
    b) Lower case without a prime (a, b) indicates the octave below Middle C (c-b). Most often these pitches are located on the second, third, and fourth strings;
    c) Upper case (E, A) indicates the second octave below Middle C (C-B). Most often these pitches are located on the fifth and sixth strings;
    d) Upper case with a prime (A´, B´) indicates the third octave below Middle C (C´-B´). Most often these pitches are located on the sixth string.
3. Roman numerals (I, VII) indicate capo position. Partial capo indications are notated thusly: **Esus** = Capo II on strings 3, 4, 5; **A** = Capo II on strings 2, 3, 4; **E6sus** = Capo II on strings 2, 3, 4, 5.
4. Plus and minus markings ("+" and "-") indicate that the strings are tuned a number of half-steps above or below concert pitch. "Standard, -2" indicates Standard tuning, lowered two half-steps.
    Actual pitches: Standard, -1 = E^b A^b d^b g^b b^b e^b´; Standard, -2 = D G c f a d´; Standard, -3 = C$^#$ F$^#$ B e g$^#$ c$^#$´; Standard, -4 = C F B^b e^b g c´.

Artists' Tunes and Tunings

TITLE	TUNING	ALBUM

SNOW, PHOEBE

Old Country Rock	Open D Capo I, or Open E^b (E^b B^b e^b g^b b^b e^b ')	Ferrington Guitars Book/CD

SONIC YOUTH

NOTE: Common tunings for Sonic Youth are: G G d g c´d´, G G B d g a, C$^\#$ F$^\#$ c$^\#$ f$^\#$ a$^\#$ b

Title	Tuning	Album
Bone	B´ E d d b b	Experimental Jet Set
Brother James	G G d d e^b´ e^b´	Bad Moon Rising
Candle	Guitar 1: A A e e a a Guitar 2: A c c g g$^\#$ c´	Daydream Nation
Cinderella's Big Score	Guitar 1: A A e e a a Guitar 2: A c c g g$^\#$ c´	Goo
Chapel Hill	Guitar 1: E G d g e d´ (second string is lower than third string) Guitar 2: E E B B e f$^\#$ (two pair of unison strings)	Dirty
Cotton Crown	G G d d e^b´ e^b´	Sister
Cross the Breeze	c c e b g d´	Daydream Nation
Death Valley '69	Guitars 1 & 2: F$^\#$ F$^\#$ f$^\#$ f$^\#$ e b (pitch of second string is below third and fourth)	Bad Moon Rising
Dirty Boots	Guitar 1: E G d g e d´ (second string is lower than third string) Guitar 2: E E B B e f$^\#$ (two pair of unison strings)	Goo
Disappearer	c c e b g d´	Goo
Eric's Trip	E B e e a b	Daydream Nation
Expressway To Yr Skull	E G$^\#$ e g$^\#$ e g$^\#$	Screaming Fields Of Sonic Love
Hey Joni	E B e e a b	Daydream Nation
Hyperstation	Guitar 1: G G d d e^b´ e^b´ Guitar 2: G G c$^\#$ d g g	
I Love Her All the Time	D$^\#$ D$^\#$ c$^\#$ c$^\#$ g g	
Kissability	E B e e a b	Goo
Kool Thing	Guitars 1 & 2: F$^\#$ F$^\#$ f$^\#$ f$^\#$ e b (pitch of second string is below third and fourth)	Goo
Mary Christ	Guitars 1 & 2: F$^\#$ F$^\#$ f$^\#$ f$^\#$ e b (pitch of second string is below third and fourth)	Goo
Mote	G G d d f f	Goo
My Friend Goo	E G d g e d´	Goo

Artists' Tunes and Tunings

TITLE	TUNING	ALBUM

Sonic Youth, continued

TITLE	TUNING	ALBUM
On the Strip	Guitars 1 & 2: $F^\#$ $F^\#$ $f^\#$ $f^\#$ e b (pitch of second string is below third and fourth)	Dirty
100%	Guitars 1 & 2: $F^\#$ $F^\#$ $f^\#$ $f^\#$ e b (pitch of second string is below third and fourth)	Dirty
Orange Rolls, Angel's Spit	G G d d $e^{b\prime}e^{b\prime}$	Dirty
Schizophrenia	$F^\#$ $F^\#$ g g a a	Sister
Screaming Skull	E G d g e d´	Experimental Jet Set
Silver Rocket	Guitar 1: A A e e $a_\#a$ Guitar 2: A c c g $g^\#$ c´	Daydream Nation
Skink	Guitar 1: B´ E d d b b Guitar 2: E G d g e d´	Experimental Jet Set
Sweet Shine	Guitar 1: E E B B e $f^\#$ Guitar 2: E G d g e d´	Experimental Jet Set
Swimsuit Issue	Guitar 1: E G d g e d´ (second string is lower than third string) Guitar 2: E E B B e $f^\#$ (two pair of unison strings)	Dirty
Theresa's Sound-World	Guitar 1: A A e e $a_\#a$ Guitar 2: A c c g $g^\#$ c´	Dirty
Titanium Expose	E G d g e d´	Goo
Tokyo Eye	E G d g e d´	
Total Trash	Guitar 1: G G $d_\#$d $e^{b\prime}e^{b\prime}$ Guitar 2: G G $c^\#$ d g g	Daydream Nation
Tunic	G G d d g g	
Teenage Riot	Guitar 1: G A B d e g Guitar 2: G G d d g g	Daydream Nation
Winner's Blues	E E B e $g^\#$ b	Experimental Jet Set
Wish Fulfillment	Guitar 1: E G d g e d´ (second string is lower than third string) Guitar 2: E E B B e $f^\#$	Dirty
Youth Against Fascism	G G d d $e^{b\prime}e^{b\prime}$	Dirty

Artists' Tunes and Tunings

TITLE	TUNING	ALBUM
SOUNDGARDEN		
Face Pollution	D A d g b b	Badmotorfinger
Mind Riot	E E e e e´	Badmotorfinger
New Damage	G6 (D G d g b e´)	Badmotorfinger
Rusty Cage	B´ A d g b e´	Badmotorfinger
Somewhere	E E B B b e´	Badmotorfinger
SOUTHER, J.D.		
Melody	Standard	Ferrington Guitars Book/CD
SPARKS, TIM		
Dance Of The Sugar Plum Fairies	Drop-D	Nutcracker Suite
SPENCE, JOSEPH		
NOTE: All recorded material in Drop-D or Drop-D, -2		
Glory Glory	Drop-D (lowered one whole-step: C G c f a d´)	Joseph Spence Folk Guitar
Won't That Be a Happy Time	Drop-D	The Real Bahamas
STANFIELD, JOHN		
Crosstie (12-String)	C G c g a c´	Moonrise
STILLS, STEPHEN		
Black Queen	D A d g b d´	Stephen Stills
Bluebird	D A d g b d´	Buffalo Springfield Again
Bluesman	E E e e b e´	Manassas
Bound To Fall	D A d g b d´	Manassas
Find The Cost Of Freedom	D A d g b d´, -2 (C G c f a c´)	So Far (CSN&Y)
4 & 20	$E^b E^b e^b e^b b^b e^b$	Deja Vu (CSN&Y)
Suite: Judy Blue Eyes	E E e e b e´ D D d d a d´	Crosby, Stills & Nash Woodstock Video
Treetop Flyer	Drop-D	
SURETTE, DAVID		
Irish Medley	D G d g c´ d´	*Fingerstyle Guitar Magazine* #8
Month of January, The	D A d g a d´	*Fingerstyle Guitar Magazine* #8

Artists' Tunes and Tunings

TITLE	TUNING	ALBUM

SWERVEDRIVER

Feel So Real	Standard, +1	Swervedriver
Kill the Superheroes	F A d a d´ e´	Swervedriver

TANANBAUM, DAVID

Jahla (by Lou Harrison)	Drop-D	The Perilous Chapel

TAYLOR, JAMES

California	Standard Capo II	Blue (Joni Mitchell)
Carolina In My Mind	Standard (D) Capo II	Greatest Hits
Copperline	Standard Capo II	Full Moon Shine
Country Road	Drop-D	Sweet Baby James
Lighthouse	Drop-D	Gorilla
Love Has Brought Me Around	Open G	Mudslide Slim
That's Why I'm Here	Standard (D) Capo III	That's Why I'm Here
You've Got A Friend	Standard (G) Capo II	Mudslide Slim; Greatest Hits

THOMPSON, ERIC

Humors of Tulla	D G d d a e´	Two Guitars (with Alan Senauke)
Skylark, The	C G d d a e	Two Guitars (with Senauke)

THOMPSON, RICHARD

NOTE: Other Richard Thompson tunings include: Open G, D G d g c´ d´, D G d g a d, F G d g c´ d´.

Banish Misfortune	D A d g a d´	The Guitar of Richard Thompson (Homespun Tapes)
Beeswing	Drop-D Capo III	Mirror Blue
Choice Wife	D A d g a d´	The Guitar of Richard Thompson
Don't Let A Thief Steal Into Your Heart	D G d g c´d´	The Guitar of Richard Thompson
I Misunderstood	Drop-D	Rumor & Sigh

__Explanation of Tunings Notation__
1. Tunings are listed from the sixth string to the first (bass to treble). Pitches listed are at the nut, not at the capo position.
2. Letter names of tunings indicate the pitch and octave of each string:
  a) Lower case with a prime (d´, e´) indicates Middle C and the octave above it (c´ - b´). Most often these pitches are located on the first string--occasionally on the second;
  b) Lower case without a prime (a, b) indicates the octave below Middle C (c-b). Most often these pitches are located on the second, third, and fourth strings;
  c) Upper case (E, A) indicates the second octave below Middle C (C-B). Most often these pitches are located on the fifth and sixth strings;
  d) Upper case with a prime (A´, B´) indicates the third octave below Middle C (C´-B´). Most often these pitches are located on the sixth string.
3. Roman numerals (I, VII) indicate capo position. Partial capo indications are notated thusly: **Esus** = Capo II on strings 3, 4, 5; **A** = Capo II on strings 2, 3, 4; **E6sus** = Capo II on strings 2, 3, 4, 5.
4. Plus and minus markings ("+" and "-") indicate that the strings are tuned a number of half-steps above or below concert pitch. "Standard, -2" indicates Standard tuning, lowered two half-steps.
  Actual pitches: Standard, -1 = E♭ A♭ d♭ g♭ b♭ e♭´; Standard, -2 = D G c f a d´; Standard, -3 = C♯ F♯ B e g♯ c♯´; Standard, -4 = C F B♭ e♭ g c´.

Artists' Tunes and Tunings

TITLE	TUNING	ALBUM
I Want To See The Bright Lights Tonight	Open G	The Guitar of Richard Thompson
Inverness Gathering	F G d g c´ d´	The Guitar of Richard Thompson
Maggie Cameron	F G d g c´ d´	The Guitar of Richard Thompson
1952 Vincent Black Lightning	C G d g b e´	Rumor & Sigh
Time To Ring Some Changes	Drop-D	The Guitar of Richard Thompson
Two Left Feet	D A d g a d´	Hand Of Kindness; Watching TheDark

THOROGOOD, GEORGE

Dixie Fried	Open G	Maverick
Gear Jammer (Slide)	Open G	Maverick
Memphis (Slide)	Open E	Maverick
What A Price	Standard Capo I	Maverick
Woman With The Blues	Open E Capo I	Maverick

TINGSTAD, ERIC

Tingstad tunings: Standard, Drop-D, D A d g b d´, Open G, C A d g b e´

Touring	D A d g b d´	Urban Guitar

TOURE, ALI FARKA

Cinquante Six	G B d g b e´	The Source

TRAUM, ARTIE

Gold Hill	Open D, Capo II (Open E)	Hard Times In The Country

TRAUM, HAPPY

Sheebeg And Sheemore	Drop-D	American Stranger
Worried Blues	Drop-D	Buckets Of Songs

VAN BERGEYK, TON

Jubilee Stomp	Drop-D	
Take It Easy	Drop-D	

VAN DUSER, GUY

Alligator Crawl	Drop-D	Stride Guitar
Boys Of Blue Hill, The	Drop-D	New Pennywhistle Album
Guitar Boogie Shuffle	Drop-D	Finger-Style Guitar Solos
Snowy Morning Blues	Drop-D	Stride Guitar

Artists' Tunes and Tunings

TITLE	TUNING	ALBUM
VAN RONK, DAVE		
Blood-Red Moon	Drop-D	Statesboro Blues; Going Back To Brooklyn
Sunday Street	Drop-D	Sunday Street
Left Banke Blues	Drop-D	Statesboro Blues; Going Back To Brooklyn
VAUGHAN, STEVIE RAY		
Cold Shot	Standard, -1 (A)	Couldn't Stand The Weather
Couldn't Stand The Weather	Standard, -1 (D)	Couldn't Stand The Weather
Honey Bee	Standard, -1 (E)	Couldn't Stand The Weather
Little Wing	Standard, -1	The Sky Is Crying
Scuttle Buttin'	Standard, -1 (E)	Couldn't Stand The Weather
Stang's Swang	Standard, -1 (F# minor)	Couldn't Stand The Weather
Voodoo Chile	Standard, -1 (E)	Couldn't Stand The Weather
WHITE, BUKKA		
Aberdeen Mississippi Blues	Open D minor	Mississippi Blues
Atlanta Special, The	Open D minor	Mississippi Blues
Baby, Please Don't Go	Open D minor	Mississippi Blues
Poor Boy Long Ways From Home	Open G, -2	
Streamline	Open D minor	Mississippi Blues
WHITE, JOSH		
John Henry	Open E	Ballads And Blues
WHITLEY, CHRIS		
Dust Radio	Open E	Living With The Law
I Forget You Every Day	Open D, -1	Living With The Law
Long Way Around	Drop-D	Living With The Law
Look What Love Has Done	Open D Capo III	Living With The Law
Phone Call From Leavenworth	Open A	Living With The Law

Explanation of Tunings Notation
1. Tunings are listed from the sixth string to the first (bass to treble). Pitches listed are at the nut, not at the capo position.
2. Letter names of tunings indicate the pitch and octave of each string:
    a) Lower case with a prime (d´, e´) indicates Middle C and the octave above it (c´ - b´). Most often these pitches are located on the first string--occasionally on the second;
    b) Lower case without a prime (a, b) indicates the octave below Middle C (c-b). Most often these pitches are located on the second, third, and fourth strings;
    c) Upper case (E, A) indicates the second octave below Middle C (C-B). Most often these pitches are located on the fifth and sixth strings;
    d) Upper case with a prime (A´, B´) indicates the third octave below Middle C (C´-B´). Most often these pitches are located on the sixth string.
3. Roman numerals (I, VII) indicate capo position. Partial capo indications are notated thusly: **Esus** = Capo II on strings 3, 4, 5; **A** = Capo II on strings 2, 3, 4; **E6sus** = Capo II on strings 2, 3, 4, 5.
4. Plus and minus markings ("+" and "-") indicate that the strings are tuned a number of half-steps above or below concert pitch. "Standard, -2" indicates Standard tuning, lowered two half-steps.
    Actual pitches: Standard, -1 = $E^b A^b d^b g^b b^b e^{b´}$; Standard, -2 = D G c f a d´; Standard, -3 = $C^{\#} F^{\#} B e g^{\#} c^{\#´}$; Standard, -4 = C F $B^b e^b$ g c´.

Artists' Tunes and Tunings

TITLE	TUNING	ALBUM
Poison Girl	Open E	Living With The Law

WILCOX, DAVID

TITLE	TUNING	ALBUM
Big Mistake	Standard Capo III + Esus V	Big Horizon
Block Dog	Open C (C G c g c e´)	Big Horizon
Break In The Cup	C G d g a d´ Capo III	Big Horizon
Burgundy Heart-Shaped Medallion	E A c$^\#$ e a c$^\#$´	Home Again
Chet Baker's Unsung Swan Song	C G d g a d´ strings 1-5 Capo V	Home Again, Rare On Live
Common As The Rain	Drop-D	How Did You Find Me Here
Covert War	C G d g a d´ Capo I + strings 1-5 V	Home Again
Farthest Shore	B´ G d f$^\#$ a d´	Big Horizon
Going Somewhere	Drop-D	Home Again
Hold It Up To The Light	Open C (C G c g c´ e´)	Big Horizon
How Did You Find Me Here	D A d e a d´ Capo IV	How Did You Find Me Here
Language Of The Heart	D A d g a d´	How Did You Find Me Here
Last Chance Waltz	Drop-D	Home Again
Please Don't Call	C G e b f c´d´	Big Horizon
That's What The Lonely Is For	C G d f$^\#$ a d´ Capo II	Big Horizon
Top Of The Rollercoaster	E^b A c$^\#$ e a b strings 1-5 IV	Home Again
Wildberry Pie	Open D	Home Again

WIJNKAMP JR, LEO

TITLE	TUNING	ALBUM
Buffalo Gals	Open G	Solos In Open Tunings (Book: S. Grossman Guitar Wkshp)
Red Wing	Open G	Solos In Open Tunings (Book)

WILLIAMSON, ROBIN

TITLE	TUNING	ALBUM
Past One O'Clock	C A d a a e´ III	Winter's Turning

YORK, ANDREW

TITLE	TUNING	ALBUM
Andecy	Drop-D	Windham Hills Sampler

YOUNG, NEIL

TITLE	TUNING	ALBUM
Cinnamon Girl	D A d g b d´	Neil Young
Ohio	D A d g b d´	So Far (CSN&Y)
When You Dance I Can Really Love	D A d g b d´	After the Goldrush

Chord Supplement

The following several pages contain fretboard diagrams for common and not-so-common chords. They are grouped together by tuning. The diagrams themselves are quite self-explanatory, with the fingered notes indicated by dots or barres. Circles on the diagrams indicate harmonics, rather than fretted notes. Please note that the chords are grouped horizontally, not vertically. Please read them left to right to follow the groupings of the chords.

You will find that many of these chord fingerings are generic, occurring in many tunes. In some cases the chords diagrammed here relate to a specific recording. For instance, the first 11 diagrams shown for Open D tuning are generic. The next seven relate directly to the Allman Brothers' classic fingerstyle tune "Little Martha." The chords are depicted in the order that they occur in the tune. Look for the original recording of "Little Martha" on the Allman Brothers' *Eat a Peach* album. Fingerstyle ace Leo Kottke recorded a version on his album *A Shout Toward Noon*. The remaining Open D chords are used by Joni Mitchell in tunes like "Chelsea Morning" and "Both Sides Now."

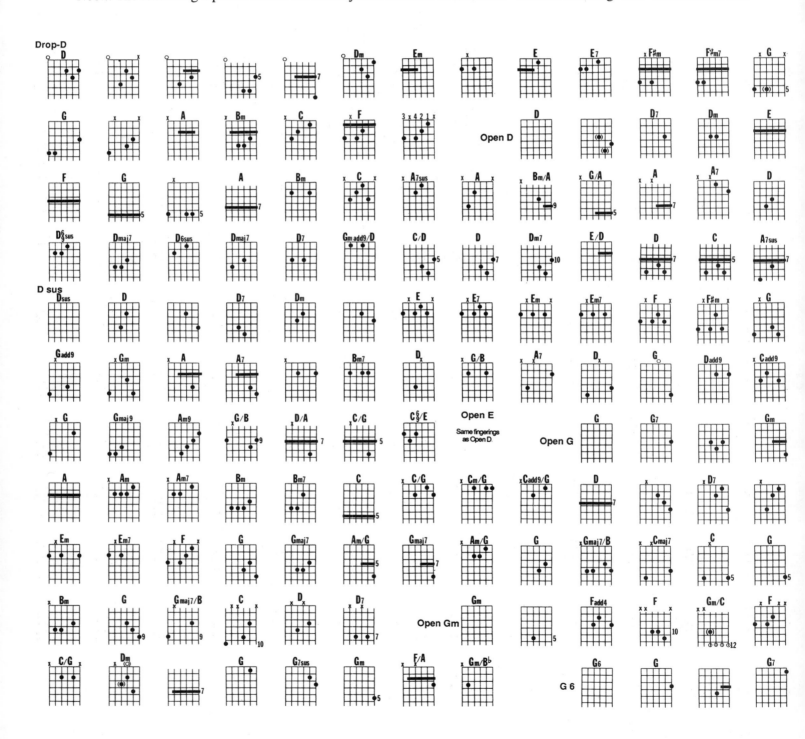

Open D: Generic through C; then "Little Martha"; then "Chelsea Morning," "Both Sides Now," and "Big Yellow Taxi," Joni Mitchell. **Dsus** (DADgad´): Generic through Bm7; then "Black Mountain Side," Jimmy Page, through Cadd9. **Open G**: Generic through Bm; then "Both Sides Now," Randy Scruggs.

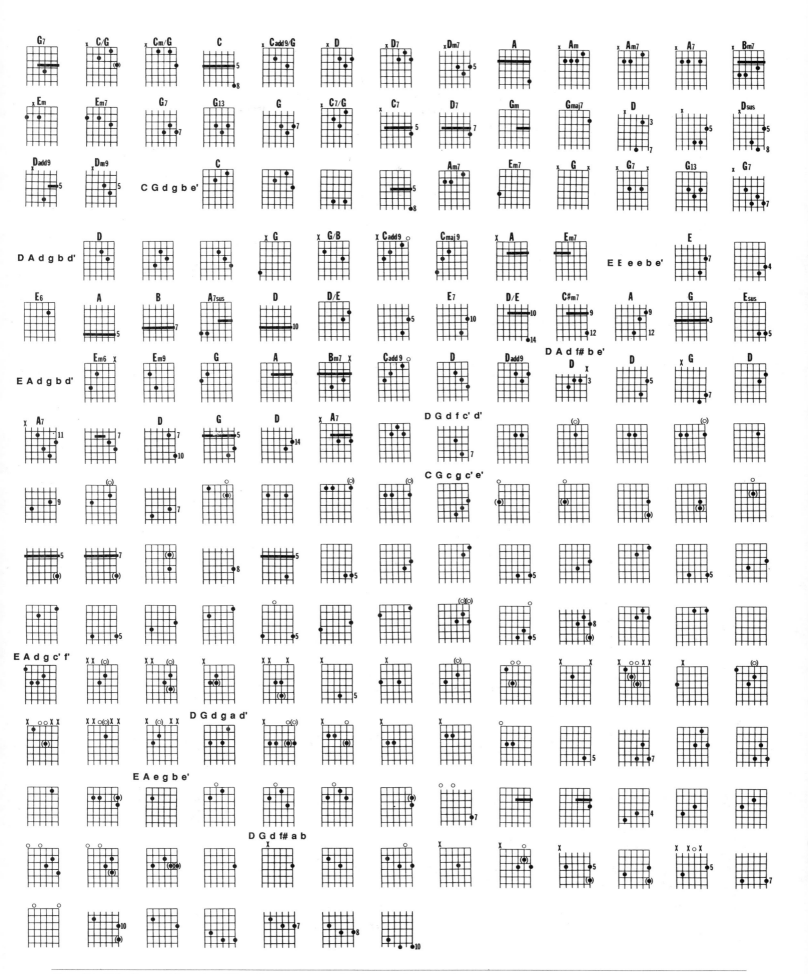

Open Gm: "Mist Covered Mountains of Home," John Renbourn. G6: Generic. C G d g b e´: "Never Going Back Again," Lindsay Buckingham. DA d g b d´: "Bluebird," Stephen Stills. EEeebe´: "Suite Judy Blue Eyes," Stephen Stills. DGdfc´d´: "Slow Motion," Wm. Ackerman. CGcgce´: "Townshend Shuffle," Wm. Ackerman. EAdgc´f´: "Bricklayer's Beautiful Daughter," Wm. Ackerman. DGdgad´: "It Takes A Year," Wm. Ackerman. EAegbe´: "Tortion Bar," Wm. Ackerman. DGdf#ab: "Pink Chiffon Tricycle," Wm. Ackerman.

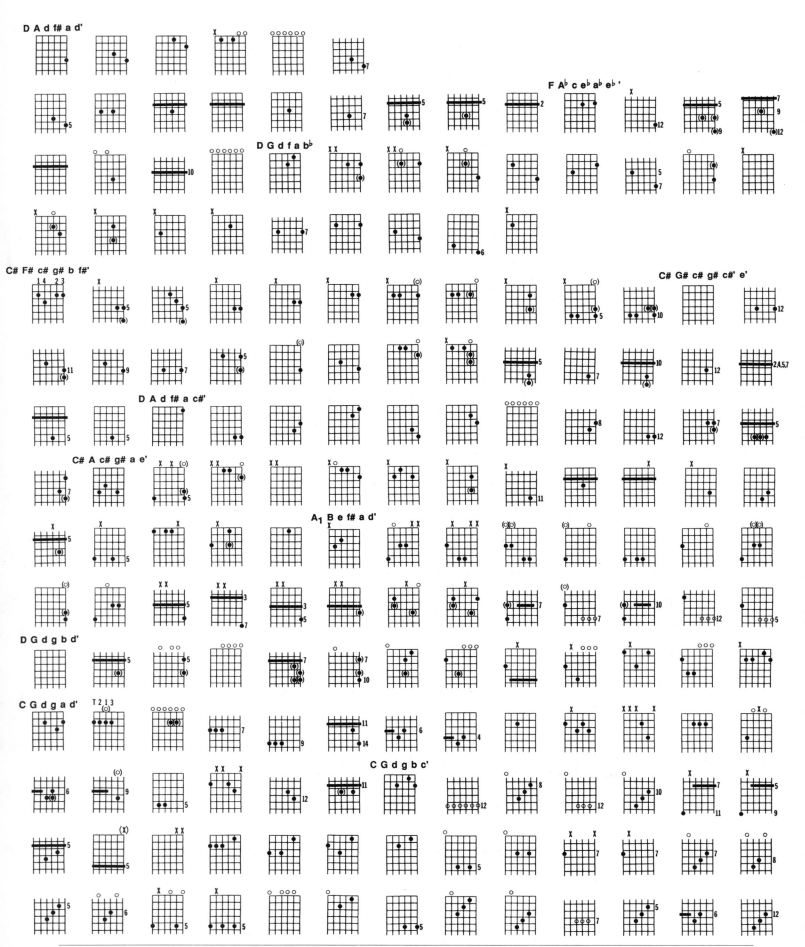

DAdf#ad´: "Ely," Wm. Ackerman. FA♭ce♭a♭be♭: "Windham Mary," Wm. Ackerman. DGdfab♭: "Processional," Wm. Ackerman. C#F#c#g#bf#´: "Buzzard," Wm. Ackerman. C#G#c#g#c#e´: Barbara's Song," Wm. Ackerman. DAdf#ac#´: "Gazos," Wm. Ackerman. C#Ac#g#ae´: "Impending Death of the Virgin Spirit," Wm. Ackerman. A´Bef#ad´: "Hot Type," Michael Hedges. DGdgbd´: "Eleven Small Roaches," Michael Hedges. CGdgad´: "Face Yourself," Michael Hedges. CGdgbc´: Rickover's Dream," Michael Hedges.

Tablature Guide

Tablature (TAB) is a notational system designed to show the instrumentalist at which fret to depress a string when plucking that string. Tablature has two main advantages over standard notation: 1) it indicates left-hand position, and 2) it is much easier to learn to read. Tablature also has its disadvantages, but for this book I recommend learning TAB if you don't read either.

Six horizontal lines represent the six strings of the guitar:

Treble:

A)

Bass:

A number on a line indicates at which fret to depress that string as you pluck it.

B)

In Ex. B, a C-chord, you pluck the strings in this order:

1) fifth string fretted at the 3rd fret,
2) second string fretted at the 1st fret,
3) fourth string fretted at the 2nd fret,
4) third string open ("0" means an open string).

The stems and beams underneath the staff denote the rhythm:

C)

Ex. C contains four eighth notes, each receiving 1/2 beat in 2/4 time. To produce the correct rhythm, count evenly "1 & 2 &" with the notes as you pluck them.

Other rhythmic markings you will see include:

o	=	whole note (full measure)	♪	=	eighth note (1/2 beat)
𝅗𝅥	=	half note (2 beats)	♪.	=	dotted eighth (3/4 beat)
𝅗𝅥.	=	dotted half note (3 beats)	♫₃	=	triplet eighths (1/3 beat each)
	=	quarter note (1 beat)	♬	=	sixteenth note (1/4 beat)
|.	=	dotted quarter (1-1/2 beats)	♬♬	=	four sixteenths (1/4 beat each)

"H" (Hammer-On), "P" (Pull-Off), and "S" (Slide) indicate notes articulated by the **left** hand.

Other Books From Mark Hanson and Accent On Music

The Art Of Contemporary Travis Picking

A comprehensive study of the patterns and variations of the modern alternating-bass fingerpicking guitar style. This book and 90-minute cassette take you from the basic patterns up through your first two solo pieces. All exercises and tunes are played at half- and full-speed on the tape. Great for beginning fingerpickers and for more advanced players who want to understand this style. 14 tunes.

The Art Of Solo Fingerpicking
Recommended by Leo Kottke and John Renbourn.

This book and 90-minute cassette thoroughly describe the intermediate-to-advanced picking techniques associated with some of today's greatest fingerpicking masters. There are 13 solo instrumentals, plus "White House Blues" from John Renbourn. All exercises and tunes are played at half- and full-speed on the tape. You'll add some hot techniques to your repertoire with this package. Formerly *Solo Style*.

Fingerstyle Noël

Our highly successful Christmas book/CD package. The 80-page book includes 30 Christmas tunes, arranged for solo fingerstyle guitar. It contains note-for-note transcriptions of ten tunes from the recording, plus an "EZ TAB" section that includes easy-to-intermediate arrangements of 20 well-known carols. The bound-in CD, entitled *Yuletide Guitar*, is a stand-alone listening recording.

Paul Simon Transcribed

Ten exact, note-for-note transcriptions from this great artist. Includes "Scarborough Fair," "Feelin' Groovy," "For Emily," "Kathy's Song," "Hearts and Bones," "Peace Like A River," and more. Standard notation/TAB, and thorough instruction for each tune.

The Music Of Leo Kottke

This book and 90-minute teaching cassette present some of Kottke's best fingerstyle guitar work in an easy-to-understand format. The note-for-note transcriptions are from Kottke's actual recordings. Mark's cassette features each entire tune played at half-speed, plus measure-by-measure instruction. TAB/standard notation. "Busted Bicycle," "Jesu, Joy," "Theme From 'The Rick & Bob Report'" and more.

Leo Kottke Transcribed

More high-quality Leo Kottke transcriptions, accompanied by Mark's measure-by-measure teaching cassette. Tunes include "William Powell," "Times Twelve," "A Trout Toward Noon," and more. Standard notation/TAB. Same format as *The Music Of Leo Kottke*.

Beginning Slide Guitar

This book tells you all you need to know about slide technique: how to set up your guitar, types of slides and hand positions, damping, fretboard "visualization," playing slide in standard and open tunings, and much more. Includes appendixes on making your own bottleneck, recommended listening, and sources for slide guitar music. *Audio Teaching Cassette available through Accent On Music*

Acoustic Jam Trax Series

Jam along with Mark and his band, the B-Street Irregulars, in this series of tapes covering a wide range of acoustic styles. Styles include acoustic blues, acoustic rock, swing, country, bluegrass, folk, and more. The accompanying books thoroughly describe how to solo over the band for each tune. Titles: *Acoustic Jam Trax, Acoustic Blues, and Acoustic Rock*. Standard notation and tablature.

12-String Guitar Guide

A great book for any guitarist interested in entering the exciting world of 12-string guitar. Guides you step-by-step through buying, stringing, and tuning your 12-string (standard and alternate tunings), and includes valuable tips on special playing techniques. Appendixes include recommended listening and reading, as well as a list of 12-string manufacturers and sources of 12-string recordings.

Distributed by Music Sales Corporation, New York, NY
For more information, inquire at your local music dealer or contact Accent On Music

Shipping & Handling Chart
Most orders are shipped within 24 hours of receipt.

	USA*	Canada/Mexico**	Europe (Airmail)	Far East/Africa (Airmail)
$24.00 and under, add	$3.95	$4.50	$10.00	$10.50
$24.01 to $50.00, add	$4.95	$5.50	$12.00	$14.00
$50.01 to $75.00, add	$5.95	$6.50	$17.00	$21.00
$75.01 to $100.00, add	$6.95	$7.50	$22.00	$28.00
$100.01 to $140.00, add	$7.95	$8.50	$28.00	$36.00
$140.01 to $200.00, add	$8.95	$9.50	$35.00	$48.00
$200.00 and over, please call				

*For USA: add $2.00 for Priority Mail. **For Canada/Mexico: add $2.50 for Priority Mail.

Order Form

• RECENT RELEASES	Catalog Number	Price
The Complete Book of Alternate Tunings	AM 7044	$16.95
Fingerstyle Noël (book & CD)	6044BK	$19.95
Yuletide Guitar (CD)	6044CD	$12.95
Yuletide Guitar (Cassette)	6044CS	$ 9.95

• ACOUSTIC MUSICIAN™ TAPE+TAB SERIES		
The Music of Leo Kottke (book & cassette)	T 301	$19.95
Leo Kottke Transcribed (book & cassette)	T 302	$19.95
Mark Hanson: Standard & Drop-D Tunings (book & cassette)	T 201	$17.95

• INSTRUCTION BOOKS		
Paul Simon Transcribed (book)	AM 4044	$19.95
The Acoustic Guitar of Martin Simpson (book)	AM 5044	$17.95
Art of Contemporary Travis Picking (book & cassette)	AM 1044	$18.95
Art of Solo Fingerpicking (formerly *Solo Style*; book & cassette)	AM 2044	$19.95

• "GUITAR CASE" SERIES		
Beginning Slide Guitar (book & cassette)	MS 020	$12.95
12-String Guitar Guide (book)	MS 030	$ 5.95
Acoustic Jam Trax (All styles: Blues, Folk, Country, Rock, Funk; book & cassette)	MS 040	$12.95
Acoustic Rock Jam Trax (Acoustic Rock; book & cassette)	MS 050	$12.95
Acoustic Blues Jam Trax (Acoustic Blues; book & cassette)	MS 060	$12.95

• COMPACT DISCS • CASSETTES • VIDEOS

We carry a variety of recordings and videos. Please call or write for a complete listing.

Catalog No.	Product	Quantity	x Unit Price	= Amount

SUBTOTAL — $_____

SHIPPING AND HANDLING: (See chart on adjoining page) — $_____

California State Sales Tax (7.25%--based on Subtotal from above). California residents only. — $_____

Add $2.00 for domestic Priority Mail (1st Class). — $_____

TOTAL: — $_____

TO ORDER:

Call (503) 699-1814, FAX (503) 699-1813, or send VISA/MASTERCARD/MONEY ORDER/CHECK (US$ drawn on a US bank), payable to:

Accent On Music, Dept. 7, 19363 Willamette Dr. #252, West Linn, OR 97068 USA.

Refund (excluding S/H) within 30 days only. Returned items must be in original condition. Opened CDs and tapes are non-returnable.

Name_____

Address_____

City_____ State_____ ZIP_____

Country_____ Telephone: Day (_____)_____ Eve (_____)_____

VISA/MC No.   ___ ___ ___ ___ - ___ ___ ___ ___ - ___ ___ ___ ___ - ___ ___ ___ ___   Exp. Date___ ___-___ ___

Signature_____

Acknowledgements

It would be impossible to list all of the people who have helped me put this project together. I have spent countless hours over several decades ferreting out tunings and fingerings from thousands of recordings. So my first thank you goes to all of the artists who have composed and recorded the superb music that has attracted and challenged me, and continues to.

My second thank you goes to my students. Since the early '70s, I have spent more countless hours working with guitar students, either deciphering recordings they bring to me that I might not have heard otherwise, or working on good musicianship, which often includes experimenting with tuner twisting. I would like to thank all of these people, past and present. You often teach me as much as I teach you.

Even after three decades of hard work (most of it fun!), I still could not have compiled such an extensive list of tunes and tunings without the assistance of many of the artists listed in the preceding pages. A hearty thank you goes to the players who provided tunings for our list. In particular, I want to thank guitarists John Renbourn, Harvey Reid, Pat Kirtley, and Martin Simpson for their interest in the project, and for the advice and suggestions they offered about its format. A big thank you for a list of Chet Atkins' tunings goes to guitar and banjo picker Jack Baker who operates the Fretted Instruments School of Folk Music in New York City. His insight into Chet Atkins' playing (clear back to the early '50s!) is considerable.

Heartfelt thanks go to computer guru Patrick Mahoney, without whose assistance this project would still be stuck in Neverland. Thanks to instigator and levity maintainer Dave McCumiskey, and to art director Chris Ledgerwood for yet another crisp cover design. Thanks to all of my publishing friends for their help, including: John Schroeter at *Fingerstyle Guitar* in Colorado Springs; David Lusterman and Dylan Schorer at *Acoustic Guitar* in San Anselmo, California; John Knowles at *Fingerstyle Quarterly* in Nashville, Tennessee; and, in particular, Andy Ellis and Joe Gore at *Guitar Player* for their help with the modern pop tunings.. Thanks again to cohorts in acoustic crime Phil Hood and Jim Hatlo for providing the opportunity. Also deserving of note are the supportive staff at Music Sales, Jim Jasmin at Digidesign, and all my friends at Gryphon Stringed Instruments (Palo Alto, Calif.), Pioneer Music (Portland, Ore.), and Dusty Strings (Seattle).

A huge debt of gratitude goes to George Winston, Keola Beamer, and all of the kind and caring folks at Dancing Cat Records in Santa Cruz, California. Their generosity with long-guarded slack key tunings information has added immeasurably to this book. Dancing Cat plans to release upwards of 60 albums in the slack key style. Your support of their endeavors in preserving this native artform for future generations would be greatly appreciated by all of us who are involved in the guitar field.

And, as always, by far my biggest debt of gratitude goes to my wife, Greta Pedersen, and my family, for effort well beyond any rational expectation. I owe them them more than one can imagine.

--*Mark Hanson*

About the Author

Mark Hanson is a well-known educator in the acoustic guitar field. He owns and operates Accent On Music, which publishes his more than one dozen guitar instruction manuals and recordings. He also is a regular columnist for *Acoustic Guitar* and *Fingerstyle Guitar* magazines. In his days as a journalist at *Frets Magazine* in the 1980s, Mark interviewed such music industry illuminaries as James Taylor, David Crosby, Larry Carlton, Jorma Kaukonen, Leo Kottke and Alex deGrassi. Mark currently lives with his family in the Pacific Northwest, and travels regularly presenting concerts and conducting guitar workshops. His first solo guitar CD, *Yuletide Guitar*, was released in 1995.